Hegel: Introduction To The

Philosophy Of History

Irwin Edman

Kessinger Publishing's Rare Reprints

Thousands of Scarce and Hard-to-Find Books on These and other Subjects!

- Americana
- Ancient Mysteries
- Animals
- Anthropology
- Architecture
- Arts
- Astrology
- Bibliographies
- Biographies & Memoirs
- Body, Mind & Spirit
- Business & Investing
- Children & Young Adult
- Collectibles
- Comparative Religions
- Crafts & Hobbies
- Earth Sciences
- Education
- Ephemera
- Fiction
- Folklore
- Geography
- Health & Diet
- History
- Hobbies & Leisure
- Humor
- Illustrated Books
- Language & Culture
- Law
- Life Sciences
- Literature
- Medicine & Pharmacy
- Metaphysical
- Music
- Mystery & Crime
- Mythology
- Natural History
- Outdoor & Nature
- Philosophy
- Poetry
- Political Science
- Science
- Psychiatry & Psychology
- Reference
- Religion & Spiritualism
- Rhetoric
- Sacred Books
- Science Fiction
- Science & Technology
- Self-Help
- Social Sciences
- Symbolism
- Theatre & Drama
- Theology
- Travel & Explorations
- War & Military
- Women
- Yoga
- *Plus Much More!*

**We kindly invite you to view our catalog list at:
http://www.kessinger.net**

Georg Wilhelm Friedrich Hegel

Hegel

THE German idealistic tradition of the early nineteenth century, of which Hegel's work was the culmination, inherited from Kant the problem of the systematization of philosophy. In this were involved two questions, one of ultimate reality and one of method; to both of these Hegel gave the fullest expositions.

For Hegel, as for Aristotle, philosophy was an encyclopaedic undertaking. Philosophy, he said, is the science of the Absolute. The Absolute is the whole of reality; Hegel speaks of it variously as absolute Reason, Idea, and Spirit or Mind. In contradistinction to Spinoza's absolute substance Hegel's Absolute may be characterized as absolute Subject. The universe of which absolute mind is the ultimate reality, is a rational system; what is rational is real and what is real is rational. A systematic description of the universe which is rational, which makes sense, is therefore true. Philosophy, therefore, may be defined as knowledge of the universe as a rational system.

True knowledge in its strictest sense could only be knowledge of the whole of reality; adequate, or to use Hegel's term, concrete, knowledge of the relations of the parts to the whole. The method of philosophy should be adapted to its subject; it should be designed to express in itself the articulation of reality. Descartes' mathematical method was adapted to a mechanical universe; Hegel's dialectic method was designed to express the organic quality of reality as he conceived it.

The relation of the parts to the whole is the definition or specification of parts within the whole. Definition is limitation, and a concrete definition is one which expresses not only the positive but also the negative aspects of this limitation. In Hegel's terms the thesis implies the antithesis and both are raised to a unity which at the same times preserves their distinctions in the synthesis. This synthesis is again a particular, a thesis which implies its antithesis and so on until the highest unity is reached in Absolute Mind.

Hegel's philosophic system, then, is the interpretation of reality in terms of this method from the most abstract undifferentiated expression in pure being to the most concrete and differentiated expression in philosophy. It represents a description of the stages of reality from the Idea in itself (Logic), the Idea for itself (Nature), to the Idea in and for itself (Mind or Spirit); the self-realization of reality, the coming to self-consciousness of mind.

The selection offered her, part of the Introduction to *The Philosophy of History,* demonstrates the application of the dialectical method and suggests the wealth of interesting and often profound insights quite apart from the value of the total system. Philosophy of history is an attempt not to gain morals from history nor to use history to prove the validity of any preconceived moral system but to interpret the meaning of the historical events themselves. The philosopher of history regards history as an involved drama and himself as a critic whose function it is to explain the plot. *The Philosophy of History* represents a compilation by Hegel's students of lectures delivered at the University of Berlin (1818-1830), where Hegel gathered about himself a large and influential group of followers.

Hegel (1770-1831) spent most of his life as professor in the universities of Jena, Heidelberg, and Berlin. During an interim of eight years after his first professorship he was editor of a newspaper and principal of a boys' school. He published only four works during his lifetime: *Phenomenology of Mind* (1807), *Science of Logic* (1812), *Encyclopaedia of the Philo-*

sophic Sciences (1817,) and *Philosophy of Right* (1821). His lectures on fine arts, religion, and the history of philosophy, as well as those on the interpretation of history, were published after his death during a cholera epidemic in 1831.

Introduction to the Philosophy of History

THE enquiry into the *essential destiny* of Reason—as far as it is considered in reference to the world—is identical with the question, *what is the ultimate purpose of the world?* And the expression implies that that purpose is to be realised. Two points of consideration suggest themselves: first, the *import* of this desgin —its abstract definition; and secondly, its *realisation.*

It must be observed at the outset, that the object we investigate —universal history—belongs to the realm of *Spirit.* The term "world," includes both physical and psychical nature. Physical nature also plays its part in the world's history, and from the very beginning attention will have to be paid to the fundamental natural relations thus involved. But Spirit, and the course of its development, is our substantial object. Our task does not require us to contemplate nature as a rational system in itself—though in its own proper domain it proves itself such—but simply in its relation to *Spirit.* On the stage on which we are observing it,— universal history—Spirit displays itself in its most concrete actuality. Notwithstanding this (or rather for the very purpose of comprehending the *general* principles which this, its form of *concrete actuality,* embodies) we must premise some abstract characteristics of the *nature of Spirit.* Such an explanation, however, cannot be given here under any other form than that of bare assertion. The present is not the occasion for unfolding the idea of Spirit speculatively; for whatever has a place in an introduction, must, as already observed, be taken as simply historical; something assumed as having been explained and proved elsewhere; or whose demonstration awaits the sequel of the Science of History itself.

We have therefore to mention here:

(1.) The abstract characteristics of the nature of Spirit.

(2.) What means Spirit uses in order to realise its Idea.

(3.) Lastly, we must consider the shape which the perfect embodiment of Spirit assumes—the state.

1] The nature of Spirit may be understood by a glance at its direct opposite—*Matter*. As the essence of matter is gravity, so, on the other hand, we may affirm that the substance, the essence of Spirit is freedom. All will readily assent to the doctrine that Spirit, among other properties, is also endowed with freedom; but philosophy teaches that all the qualities of Spirit exist only through freedom; that all are but means for attaining freedom; that all seek and produce this and this alone. It is a perception of speculative philosophy, that freedom is the sole truth of Spirit. Matter possesses gravity in virtue of its tendency towards a central point. It is essentially composite; consisting of parts that *exclude* each other. It seeks its unity; and therefore exhibits the tendency towards self-destruction, towards its opposite [an indivisible point]. If it could attain this, it would be matter no longer, it would have perished. It strives after the realisation of its Idea; for in unity it exists *ideally*. Spirit, on the contrary, may be defined as that which has its centre in itself. It has not a unity beyond itself, but has already found it; it exists *in* and *with itself*. Matter has its essence out of itself; Spirit is *self-contained existence* (Bei-sich-selbst-seyn). Now this is freedom, exactly. For if I am dependent, my being is referred to something else which I am not; I cannot exist independently of something external. I am free, on the contrary, when my existence depends upon myself. This self-contained existence of Spirit is none other than self-consciousness—consciousness of one's own being. Two things must be distinguished in consciousness; first, the fact *that I know;* secondly, *what I know.* In *self* consciousness these are merged in one; for Spirit *knows itself.* It involves an appreciation of its own nature, as also an energy enabling it to realise itself; to make itself *actually* that which it is *potentially.* According to this abstract definition it may be said of universal history, that it is the exhibition of Spirit in the process of working out the knowledge of that which it is potentially. And as the germ bears in itself the whole nature of

the tree, and the taste and form of its fruits, so do the first traces
of Spirit virtually contain the whole of that history. The Orientals
have not attained the knowledge that Spirit—Man *as such*—is free;
and because they do not know this they are not free. They only
know that *one is free*. But on this very account, the freedom of
that one is only caprice; ferocity—brutal recklessness or passion,
or a mildness and tameness of the desires, which is itself only an
accident of nature or mere caprice like the former.—That *one* is
therefore only a despot; not a *free man*. The consciousness of
freedom first arose among the Greeks, and therefore they were
free; but they, and the Romans likewise, knew only that *some* are
free,—not man as such. Even Plato and Aristotle did not know
this. The Greeks, therefore, had slaves; and their whole life and
the maintenance of their splendid liberty, was implicated with
the institution of slavery: a fact moreover, which made that
liberty on the one hand only an accidental, transient and limited
growth; on the other hand, constituted it a rigorous thraldom of
our common nature—of the human. The German nations, under
the influence of Christianity, were the first to attain the consciousness, that man, as man, is free: that it is the *freedom* of Spirit
which constitutes its essence. This consciousness arose first in
religion, the inmost region of Spirit; but to introduce the principle
into the various relations of the actual world, involves a more
extensive problem than its simple implantation; a problem whose
solution and application require a severe and lengthened process
of culture. As an example of this, we may note that slavery did
not cease immediately on the reception of Christianity. Still less
did liberty predominate in states; or governments and constitutions adopt a rational organization, or recognise freedom as their
basis. That application of the principle to political relations; the
thorough moulding and interpenetration of the constitution of
society by it, is a process identical with history itself. I have already
directed attention to the distinction here involved, between a
principle as such, and its *application;* *i.e.* its introduction and
carrying out in the actuality of Spirit and life. This is a point of
fundamental importance in our science, and one which must be
constantly respected as essential. And in the same way as this distinction has attracted attention in view of the *Christian* principle
of self-consciousness—freedom; it also shews itself as an essential

one, in view of the principle of freedom *generally*. The history of the world is none other than the progress in the consciousness of freedom; a progress whose development according to the necessity of its nature, it is our business to investigate.

The general statement given above, of the various grades in the consciousness of freedom—and which we applied in the first instance to the fact that the Eastern nations knew only that *one* is free; the Greek and Roman world only that *some* are free; whilst *we* know that all men absolutely (man *as man*) are free,—supplies us with the natural division of universal history, and suggests the mode of its discussion. This is remarked, however, only incidentally and anticipatively; some other ideas must be first explained.

The destiny of the spiritual world, and,—since this is the *substantial world,* while the physical remains subordinate to it, or, in the language of speculation, has no truth *as against* the spiritual, —the *final cause of the world at large,* we allege to be the *consciousness* of its own freedom on the part of Spirit, and *ipso facto,* the *reality* of that freedom. But that this term "freedom," without further qualification, is an indefinite, and incalculable ambiguous term; and that while that which it represents is the *ne plus ultra* of attainment, it is liable to an infinity of misunderstandings, confusions and errors, and to become the occasion for all imaginable excesses,—has never been more clearly known and felt than in modern times. Yet, for the present, we must content ourselves with the term itself without farther definition. Attention was also directed to the importance of the infinite difference between a principle in the abstract, and its actualization in the concrete. In the process before us, the essential nature of freedom—which involves in it absolute necessity,—is to be displayed as coming to a consciousness of itself (for it is in its very nature, self-consciousness) and thereby actualizing its existence. Itself is its own object of attainment, and the sole aim of Spirit. This result it is, at which the process of the world's history has been continually aiming; and to which the sacrifices that have ever and anon been laid on the vast altar of the earth, through the long lapse of ages, have been offered. This is the only aim that sees itself realised and fulfilled; the only pole of repose amid the ceaseless change of events and conditions, and the truly efficient principle that pervades them. This final aim is God's purpose with the world; but

God is the absolutely perfect being, and can, therefore, will nothing other than himself—his own will. The nature of His will—that is, His nature itself—is what we here call the idea of freedom; translating the language of religion into that of thought. The question, then, which we may next put, is: What means does this principle of freedom use for its realisation? This is the second point we have to consider.

2] The question of the *means* by which freedom develops itself to a world, conducts us to the phenomenon of history itself. Although freedom is, primarily, an undeveloped idea, the means it uses are external and phenomenal; presenting themselves in history to our sensuous vision. The first glance at history convinces us that the actions of men proceed from their needs, their passions, their interests, their characters and talents; and impresses us with the belief that such needs, passions and interests are the sole springs of action—the efficient agents in this scene of activity. Among these may, perhaps, be found aims of a liberal or universal kind—benevolence it may be, or noble patriotism; but such virtues and general views are but insignificant as compared with the world and its doings. We may perhaps see the ideal of Reason actualized in those who adopt such aims, and within the spheres of their influence; but they bear only a trifling proportion to the mass of the human race; and the extent of that influence is limited accordingly. Passions, private aims, and the satisfaction of selfish desires, are on the other hand, most effective springs of action. Their power lies in the fact that they respect none of the limitations which justice and morality would impose on them; and that these natural impulses have a more direct influence over man than the artificial and tedious discipline that tends to order and self-restraint, law and morality. When we look at this display of passions, and the consequences of their violence; the unreason which is associated not only with them, but even (rather we might say *especially*) with *good* designs and righteous aims; when we see the evil, the vice, the ruin that has befallen the most flourishing kingdoms which the mind of man ever created, we can scarce avoid being filled with sorrow at this universal taint of corruption: and, since this decay is not the work of mere nature, but of the human will—a moral embitterment—a revolt of the good spirit (if it have a place within us) may well be the result of our reflections. Without rhetorical exaggeration, a simply truthful combination of the miseries that have overwhelmed the noblest of nations and polities, and the finest exemplars of private virtue,—forms a picture of most fearful aspect, and excites emotions of the profoundest and most hopeless sadness, counter-balanced by no consolatory result. We endure in beholding it a mental torture, allowing no defence or escape but the consideration that what has happened could not be otherwise; that it is a fatality which no intervention could alter. And at last we draw back from the intolerable disgust with which these sorrowful reflections threaten us, into the more agreeable environment of our individual life—the present formed by our private aims and interests. In short we retreat into the selfishness that stands on the quiet shore, and thence enjoy in safety the distant spectacle of "wrecks confusedly hurled." But even regarding history as the slaughter-bench at which the happiness of peoples, the wisdom of states, and the virtue of individuals have been victimised—the question involuntarily arises—to what principle, to what final aim these enormous sacrifices have been offered. From this point the investigation usually proceeds to that which we have made the general commencement of our enquiry. Starting from this we pointed out those events which made up a picture so suggestive of gloomy emotions and thoughtful reflections—as *the very field* which we, for our part, regard as exhibiting only the means for realising what we assert to be the essential destiny—the absolute aim, or—which comes to the same thing—the true *result* of the world's history. We have all along purposely eschewed "moral reflections" as a method of rising from the scene of particular historical events to the general principles which they embody. Besides, it is not the interest of such sentimentalities, really to rise above those depressing emotions; and to solve the enigmas of providence which the considerations that occasioned them, present. It is essential to their character to find a gloomy satisfaction in the empty and fruitless sublimities of that negative result. We return then to the point of view which we have adopted; observing that the successive steps (Momente) of the analysis to which it will lead us, will also evolve the conditions requisite for answering the enquiries suggested by the panorama of sin and suffering that history unfolds.

The *first* remark we have to make, and which—though already presented more than once—cannot be too often repeated when the occasion seems to call for it,—is that what we call *principle, aim, destiny,* or the nature and idea of Spirit, is something merely general and abstract. Principle—plan of existence—law—is an undeveloped essence, which *as such*—however true in itself—is not completely actual. Aims, principles, &c., have a place in our thoughts, in our subjective design only; but not yet in the sphere of actuality. That which exists for itself only, is a possibility, a potentiality; but has not yet emerged into existence. A *second* element must be introduced in order to produce actuality—viz. actuation, realization; and whose principle is the will—the activity of man in the widest sense. It is only by this activity that that Idea as well as abstract characteristics generally, are realised, actualised; for of themselves they are powerless. The motive power that puts them in operation, and gives them determinate existence, is the need, instinct, inclination, and passion of man. That some conception of mine should be developed into act and existence, is my earnest desire: I wish to assert my personality in connection with it: I wish to be satisfied by its execution. If I am to exert myself for any object, it must in some way or other be *my* object. In the accomplishment of such or such designs I must at the same time find *my* satisfaction; although the purpose for which I exert myself includes a complication of results, many of which have no interest for me. This is the absolute right of personal existence—to find *itself* satisfied in its activity and labour. If men are to interest themselves for anything, they must (so to speak) have part of their existence involved in it; find their individuality gratified by its attainment. Here a mistake must be avoided. We intend blame, and justly impute it as a fault, when we say of an individual, that he is "interested" (in taking part in such or such transactions) that is, seeks only his private advantage. In reprehending this we find fault with him for furthering his personal aims without any regard to a more comprehensive design; of which he takes advantage to promote his own interest, or which he even sacrifices with this view. But he who is active in *promoting an object,* is not simply "interested," but interested in that object itself. Language faithfully expresses this distinction.—Nothing therefore happens, nothing is accomplished, unless the individuals concerned, seek their own satisfaction in the issue. They are particular units of society; *i.e.* they have special needs, instincts, and interests generally, peculiar to themselves. Among these needs are not only such as we usually call necessities—the stimuli of individual desire and volition—but also those connected with individual views and convictions; or—to use a term expressing less decision—leanings of opinion; supposing the impulses of reflection, understanding, and reason, to have been awakened. In these cases people demand, if they are to exert themselves in any direction, that the object should commend itself to them; that in point of opinion,—whether as to its goodness, justice, advantage, profit,—they should be able to "enter into it" (dabei seyn). This is a consideration of especial importance in our age, when people are less than formerly influenced by reliance on others, and by authority; when, on the contrary, they devote their activities to a cause on the ground of their own understanding, their independent conviction and opinion.

We assert then that nothing has been accomplished without interest on the part of the actors; and—if interest be called passion, inasmuch as the whole individuality, to the neglect of all other actual or possible interests and aims, is devoted to an object with every fibre of volition, concentrating all its desires and powers upon it—we may affirm absolutely that *nothing great* in *the world* has been accomplished without *passion*. Two elements, therefore, enter into the object of our investigation; the first the Idea, the second the complex of human passions; the one the warp, the other the woof of the vast tapestry of universal history. The concrete mean and union of the two is liberty, under the conditions of morality in a state. We have spoken of the idea of freedom as the nature of Spirit, and the absolute goal of history. Passion is regarded as a thing of sinister aspect, as more or less immoral. Man is required to have no passions. Passion, it is true, is not quite the suitable word for what I wish to express. I mean here nothing more than human activity as resulting from private interests—special, or if you will, self-seeking designs—with this qualification, that the whole energy of will and character is devoted to their attainment; that other interests (which would in themselves constitute attractive aims), or rather all things else, are sacrificed to them. The object in question is so bound up with the man's will, that it entirely and alone determines the "hue of resolution," and

is inseparable from it. It has become the very essence of his volition. For a person is a specific existence; not man in general (a
term to which no real existence corresponds), but a particular
human being. The term "character" likewise expresses this idiosyncrasy of will and intelligence. But *character* comprehends all
peculiarities whatever; the way in which a person conducts himself
in private relations, &c., and is not limited to his idiosyncrasy in
its practical and active phase. I shall, therefore, use the term "passion"; understanding thereby the particular bent of character, as
far as the peculiarities of volition are not limited to private interest, but supply the impelling and actuating force for accomplishing
deeds shared in by the community at large. Passion is in the first
instance the *subjective*, and therefore the *formal* side of energy,
will, and activity—leaving the object or aim still undetermined.
And there is a similar relation of formality to reality in merely
individual conviction, individual views, individual conscience. It
is always a question, of essential importance, what is the purport
of my conviction, what the object of my passion, in deciding
whether the one or the other is of a true and substantial nature.
Conversely, if it is so, it will inevitably attain actual existence—be
actualized.

From this comment on the second essential element in the historical embodiment of an aim, we infer—glancing at the institution of the state in passing—that a state is then well constituted and
internally powerful, when the private interest of its citizens is one
with the common interest of the state; when the one finds its gratification and realization in the other,—a proposition in itself very
important. But in a state many institutions must be adopted, much
political machinery invented, accompanied by appropriate political arrangements,—necessitating long struggles of the understanding before what is really appropriate can be discovered,—involving,
moreover, contentions with private interest and passions, and a
tedious discipline of these latter, in order to bring about the desired harmony. The epoch when a state attains this harmonious
condition, marks the period of its bloom, its virtue, its vigour, and
its prosperity. But the history of mankind does not begin with a
conscious aim of any kind, as it is the case with the particular
circles into which men form themselves of set purpose. The mere
social instinct implies a conscious purpose of security for life and

property; and when society has been constituted, this purpose becomes more comprehensive. The history of the world begins with its general aim—the realization of the idea of Spirit—only in an *implicit* form *(an sich)* that is, as nature; an inmost, unconscious instinct; and the whole process of history (as already observed), is directed to rendering this unconscious impulse a conscious one. Thus appearing in the form of merely natural existence, natural will—that which has been called the subjective side,—physical craving, instinct, passion, private interest, as also opinion and subjective conception,—spontaneously present themselves at the very commencement. This vast congeries of volitions, interests and activities, constitute the instruments and means of the world-spirit for attaining its object; bringing it to consciousness, and realising it. And this aim is none other than finding itself—coming to itself—and contemplating itself in concrete actuality. But that those manifestations of vitality on the part of individuals and peoples, in which they seek and satisfy their own purposes, are, at the same time, the means and instruments of a higher and broader purpose of which they know nothing,—which they realise unconsciously,—might be made a matter of question; rather has been questioned, and in every variety of form negatived, decried and contemned as mere dreaming and "philosophy." But on this point I announced my view at the very outset, and asserted our hypothesis,—which, however, will appear in the sequel, in the form of a legitimate inference,—and our belief, that Reason governs the world, and has consequently governed its history. In relation to this independently universal and substantial existence—all else is subordinate, subservient to it, and the means for its development. But moreover this Reason is immanent in historical existence and attains to its own perfection in and through that existence. The union of universal abstract existence generally with the individual, —the subjective—that this alone is truth, belongs to the department of speculation, and is treated in this general form in logic.— But in the process of the world's history itself,—as still incomplete, —the abstract final aim of history is not yet made the distinct object of desire and interest. While these limited sentiments are still unconscious of the purpose they are fulfilling, the universal principle is implicit in them, and is realizing itself through them. The question also assumes the form of the union of *freedom and neces-*

sity; the latent abstract process of Spirit being regarded as *necessity,* while that which exhibits itself in the conscious will of men, as their interest, belongs to the domain of *freedom.* As the metaphysical connection (*i.e.* the connection in the Idea) of these forms of thought, belongs to logic, it would be out of place to analyse it here. The chief and cardinal points only shall be mentioned.

Philosophy shows that the Idea advances to an infinite antithesis; that, viz. between the Idea in its free, universal form—in which it exists for itself—and the contrasted form of abstract introversion, reflection on itself, or formal self-existence, ego, formal freedom, such as belongs to Spirit only. The universal Idea exists thus as the substantial totality of things on the one side, and as the abstract essence of free volition on the other side. This reflection of the mind on itself is individual self-consciousness—the polar opposite of the Idea in its general form, and therefore existing in absolute limitation. This polar opposite is consequently limitation, particularization, for the universal absolute being; it is the side of its *definite existence;* the sphere of its formal reality, the sphere of the reverence paid to God.—To comprehend the absolute connection of this antithesis, is the profound task of metaphysics. This limitation originates all forms of particularity of whatever kind. The formal volition [of which we have spoken] wills itself; desires to make its own personality valid in all that it purposes and does: even the pious individual wishes to be saved and happy. This pole of the anthithesis, existing for itself, is—in contrast with the absolute universal being—a special separate existence, taking cognizance of speciality only, and willing that alone. In short it plays its part in the region of mere phenomena. This is the sphere of particular purposes, in effecting which individuals exert themselves on behalf of their individuality—give it full play and objective actualization. This is also the sphere of happiness and its opposite. He is happy who finds his condition suited to his special character, will, and fancy, and so enjoys himself in that condition. The history of the world is not the theatre of happiness. Periods of happiness are blank pages in it, for they are periods of harmony,—periods when the antithesis is in abeyance. Reflection on self,—the freedom above described—is abstractly defined as the formal element of the activity of the absolute Idea. The realizing *activity* of which we have spoken is the middle term of the syllogism, one of whose extremes is the universal essence, the *Idea*, which reposes in the penetralia of Spirit; and the other, the complex of external things, objective matter. That activity is the medium by which the universal latent principle is translated into the domain of objectivity.

I will endeavour to make what has been said more vivid and clear by examples.

The building of a house is, in the first instance, a subjective aim and design. On the other hand we have, as means, the several substances required for the work,—iron, wood, stones. The elements are made use of in working up this material: fire to melt the iron, wind to blow the fire, water to set wheels in motion, in order to cut the wood, &c. The result is, that the wind, which has helped to build the house, is shut out by the house; so also are the violence of rains and floods, and the destructive powers of fire, so far as the house is made fire-proof. The stones and beams obey the law of gravity,—press downwards,—and so high walls are carried up. Thus the elements are made use of in accordance with their nature, and yet co-operate for a product, by which their operation is limited. Thus the passions of men are gratified; they develop themselves and their aims in accordance with their natural tendencies, and build up the edifice of human society; thus fortifying a position for right and order *against themselves*.

The connection of events above indicated, involves also the fact, that in history an additional result is commonly produced by human actions beyond that which they aim at and obtain—that which they immediately recognise and desire. They gratify their own interest; but something farther is thereby accomplished, latent in the actions in question, though not present to their consciousness, and not included in their design. An analogous example is offered in the case of a man who, from a feeling of revenge,—perhaps not an unjust one, but produced by injury on the other's part,—burns that other man's house. A connection is immediately established between the deed itself and a train of circumstances not directly included in it, taken abstractedly. In itself it consisted in merely presenting a small flame to a small portion of a beam. Events not involved in that simple act follow of themselves. The part of the beam which was set fire to is connected with its remote portions; the beam itself is united with the woodwork of the house generally, and this with other houses; so that a wide conflagration ensues, which destroys the goods and chattels of many other persons besides his against whom the act of revenge was first directed; perhaps even costs not a few men their lives. This lay neither in the deed abstractedly, nor in the design of the man who committed it. But the action has a further general bearing. In the design of the doer it was only revenge executed against an individual in the destruction of his property, but it is moreover a crime, and that involves punishment also. This may not have been present to the mind of the perpetrator, still less in his intention; but his deed itself, the general principles it calls into play, its substantial content entails it. By this example I wish only to impress on you the consideration, that in a simple act, something further may be implicated than lies in the intention and consciousness of the agent. The example before us involves, however, this additional consideration, that the substance of the act, consequently we may say the act itself, recoils upon the perpetrator,—reacts upon him with destructive tendency. This union of the two extremes—the embodiment of a general idea in the form of direct actuality, and the elevation of a particularity into connection with universal truth— is brought to pass, at first sight, under the conditions of an utter diversity of nature between the two, and an indifference of the one extreme towards the other. The aims which the agents set before them are limited and special; but it must be remarked that the agents themselves are intelligent thinking beings. The purport of their aims is interwoven with *general, essential* considerations of justice, good, duty, &c.; for mere desire—volition in its rough and savage forms—falls not within the scene and sphere of universal history. Those general considerations, which form at the same time a norm for directing aims and actions, have a determinate purport; for such an abstraction as "good for its own sake," has no place in living actuality. If men are to act, they must not only intend the good, but must have decided for themselves whether this or that particular thing is a good. What special course of action, however, is good or not, is determined, as regards the ordinary contingencies of private life, by the laws and customs of a state; and here no great difficulty is presented. Each individual has his position; he knows on the whole what a just, honourable course of conduct is. As to ordinary, private relations, the assertion that it is difficult to choose the right and good,—the regarding it as the mark of an exalted morality to find difficulties and raise scruples on that score, —may be set down to an evil or perverse will, which seeks to evade duties not in themselves of a perplexing nature; or, at any rate, to an idly reflective habit of mind—where a feeble will affords no sufficient exercise to the faculties,—leaving them therefore to find occupation within themselves, and to expend themselves on moral self-adulation.

It is quite otherwise with the comprehensive relations that history has to do with. In this sphere are presented those momentous collisions between existing, acknowledged duties, laws, and rights, and those contingencies which are adverse to this fixed system; which assail and even destroy its foundations and existence; whose tenor may nevertheless seem good,—on the large scale advantageous,—yes, even indispensable and necessary. These contingencies realise themselves in history: they involve a general principle of a different order from that on which depends the *permanence* of a people or a state. This principle is an essential phase in the development of the *creating* Idea, of truth striving and urging towards [consciousness of] itself. Historical men—*world-historical individuals*—are those in whose aims such a general principle lies.

Caesar, in danger of losing a position, not perhaps at that time of superiority, yet at least of equality with the others who were at the head of the state, and of succumbing to those who were just on the point of becoming his enemies,—belongs essentially to this category. These enemies—who were at the same time pursuing *their* personal aims—had the form of the constitution, and the power conferred by an appearance of justice, on their side. Caesar was contending for the maintenance of his position, honour, and safety; and, since the power of his opponents included the sovereignty over the provinces of the Roman Empire, his victory secured for him the conquest of that entire empire; and he thus became—though leaving the form of the constitution—the autocrat of the state. That which secured for him the execution of a design, which in the first instance was of negative import—the autocracy of Rome,—was, however, at the same time an independently necessary feature in the history of Rome and of the world. It was not, then, his private gain merely, but an unconscious impulse that occasioned the accomplishment of that for which the time was ripe. Such are all great historical men,—whose own particular aims, involve those large issues which are the will of the world-spirit. They may be called heroes, inasmuch as they have derived their purposes and their vocation, not from the calm, regular course of things, sanctioned by the existing order; but from a concealed fount—one which has not attained to phenomenal, present existence,—from that inner Spirit, still hidden beneath the surface, which, impinging on the outer world as on a shell, bursts it in pieces, because it is another kernel than that which belonged to the shell in question. They are men, therefore, who appear to draw the impulse of their life from themselves; and whose deeds have produced a condition of things and a complex of historical relations which appear to be only *their* interest, and *their* work.

Such individuals had no consciousness of the general Idea they were unfolding, while prosecuting those aims of theirs; on the contrary, they were practical, political men. But at the same time they were thinking men, who had an insight into the requirements of the time—*what was ripe for development.* This was the very truth for their age, for their world; the species next in order, so to speak, and which was already formed in the womb of time. It was theirs to know this nascent principle; the necessary, directly sequent step in progress, which their world was to take; to make this their aim, and to expend their energy in promoting it. World-historical men—the heroes of an epoch—must, therefore, be recognised as its clear-sighted ones; *their* deeds, *their* words are the best of that time. Great men have formed purposes to satisfy themselves, not others. Whatever prudent designs and counsels they might have learned from others, would be the more limited and inconsistent features in their career; for it was they who best understood affairs; from whom *others* learned, and approved, or at least acquiesced in —their policy. For that Spirit which had taken this fresh step in history is the inmost soul of all individuals; but in a state of unconsciousness which the great men in question aroused. Their fellows, therefore, follow these soul-leaders; for they feel the irresistible power of their own inner spirit thus embodied. If we go on to cast a look at the fate of these world-historical persons, whose vocation it was to be the agents of the world-spirit,—we shall find it to have been no happy one. They attained no calm enjoyment; their whole life was labour and trouble; their whole nature was nought else but their master-passion. When their object is attained they fall off like empty hulls from the kernel. They die early, like Alexander; they are murdered, like Caesar; transported to St. Helena, like Napoleon. This fearful consolation—that historical men have not enjoyed what is called happiness, and of which only private life (and this may be passed under very various external circumstances) is capable,—this consolation those may draw from history, who stand in need of it; and it is craved by envy—vexed at what is great and transcendant,—striving, therefore, to depreciate it, and to find some flaw in it. Thus in modern times it has been demonstrated *ad nauseam* that princes are generally unhappy on their thrones; in consideration of which the possession of a throne is tolerated, and men acquiesce in the fact that not themselves but the personages in question are its occupants. The free man, we may observe, is not envious, but gladly recognises what is great and exalted, and rejoices that it exists.

It is in the light of those common elements which constitute the interest and therefore the passions of individuals, that these historical men are to be regarded. They are *great* men, because they willed and accomplished something great; not a mere fancy, a mere intention, but that which met the case and fell in with the needs of the age. This mode of considering them also excludes the so-called "psychological" view, which—serving the purpose of envy most effectually—contrives so to refer all actions to the heart,—to bring them under such a subjective aspect—as that their authors appear to have done everything under the impulse of some passion, mean or grand,—some *morbid craving,*—and on account of these passions and cravings to have been not moral men. Alexander of Macedon partly subdued Greece, and then Asia; therefore he was possessed by a *morbid craving* for conquest. He is alleged to have acted from a craving for fame, for conquest; and the proof that these were the impelling motives is that he did that which resulted in fame. What pedagogue has not demonstrated of Alexander the Great—of Julius Caesar—that they were instigated by such passions, and were consequently immoral men?—whence the conclusion immediately follows that he, the pedagogue, is a better man than they, because he has not such passions; a proof of which lies in the fact that he does not conquer Asia,—vanquish Darius and Porus,—but while he enjoys life himself lets others enjoy it too.

These psychologists are particularly fond of contemplating those peculiarities of great historical figures which appertain to them as private persons. Man must eat and drink; he sustains relations to friends and acquaintances; he has passing impulses and ebullitions of temper. "No man is a hero to his valet-de-chambre," is a well-known proverb; I have added—and Goethe repeated it ten years later—"but not because the former is no hero, but because the latter is a valet." He takes off the hero's boots, assists him to bed, knows that he prefers champagne, &c. Historical personages waited upon in historical literature by such psychological valets, come poorly off; they are brought down by these their attendants to a level with—or rather a few degrees below the level of—the morality of such exquisite discerners of spirits. The Thersites of Homer who abuses the kings is a standing figure for all times. Blows—that is beating with a solid cudgel—he does not get in every age, as in the Homeric one; but his envy, his egotism, is the thorn which he has to carry in his flesh; and the undying worm that gnaws him is the tormenting consideration that his excellent views and vituperations remain absolutely without result in the world. But our satisfaction at the fate of thersitism also, may have its sinister side.

A world-historical individual is not so unwise as to indulge a variety of wishes to divide his regards. He is devoted to the one aim, regardless of all else. It is even possible that such men may treat other great, even sacred interests, inconsiderately; conduct which is indeed obnoxious to moral reprehension. But so mighty a form must trample down many an innocent flower—crush to pieces many an object in its path.

The special interest of passion is thus inseparable from the active development of a general principle: for it is from the special and determinate and from its negation, that the universal results. Particularity contends with its like, and some loss is involved in the issue. *It* is not the general idea that is implicated in opposition and combat, and that is exposed to danger. It remains in the background, untouched and uninjured. This may be called the *cunning of reason*,—that it sets the passions to work for itself, while that which develops its existence through such impulsion pays the penalty, and suffers loss. For it is *phenomenal* being that is so treated, and of this, part is of no value, part is positive and real. The particular is for the most part of too trifling value as compared with the general: individuals are sacrificed and abandoned. The Idea pays the penalty of determinate existence and of corruptibility, not from itself, but from the passions of individuals.

But though we might tolerate the idea that individuals, their desires and the gratification of them, are thus sacrificed, and their happiness given up to the empire of chance, to which it belongs; and that as a general rule, individuals come under the category of means to an ulterior end,—there is one aspect of human individuality which we should hesitate to regard in that subordinate light, even in relation to the highest; since it is absolutely no subordinate element, but exists in those individuals as inherently eternal and divine. I mean *morality, ethics, religion*. Even when speaking of the realization of the great ideal aim by means of individuals, the *subjective* element in them—their interest and that of their cravings and impulses, their views and judgments, though exhibited as the merely formal side of their existence,—was spoken of as having an infinite right to be consulted. The first idea that presents itself in speaking of *means* is that of something external to the object, and having no share in the object itself. But merely natural things—even the commonest lifeless objects—used as means, must be of such a kind as adapts them to their purpose; they must possess something in common with it. Human beings least of all, sustain the bare external relation of mere means to the great ideal aim. Not only do they in the very act of realising it, make it the occasion of satisfying personal desires, whose purport is diverse from that aim—but they share in that ideal aim itself; and are for that very reason objects of their own existence; not *formally* merely, as the world of living beings generally is—whose individual life is essentially subordinate to that of man, and is properly used *up* as an instrument. Men, on the contrary, are objects of existence to themselves, as regards the intrinsic import of the aim in question. To this order belongs that in them which we would exclude from the category of mere means,—morality, ethics, religion. That is to say, man is an object of existence in himself only in virtue of the divine that is in him,—that which was designated at the outset as *Reason;* which, in view of its activity and power of self-determination, was called *freedom*. And we affirm—without entering at present on the proof of the assertion—that religion, morality, &c. have their foundation and source in that principle, and so are essentially elevated above all alien necessity and chance. And here we must remark that individuals, to the extent of their freedom, are responsible for the depravation and enfeeblement of morals and religion. This is the seal of the absolute and sublime destiny of man—that he knows what is good and what is evil; that his destiny *is* his very ability to will either good or evil,—in one word, that he is the subject of moral imputation, imputation not only of evil, but of good; and not only concerning this or that particular matter, and all that happens *ab extrâ*, but *also* the good and evil attaching to his individual freedom. The brute alone is simply innocent. It would, however, demand an extensive explanation—as extensive as the analysis of moral freedom itself—to preclude or obviate all the misunderstandings which the statement that what is called innocent imports the entire unconsciousness of evil—is wont to occasion.

In contemplating the fate which virtue, morality, even piety experience in history, we must not fall into the litany of lamentations, that the good and pious often—or for the most part—fare ill in the world, while the evil-disposed and wicked prosper. The term *prosperity* is used in a variety of meanings—riches, outward honour, and the like. But in speaking of something which in and for itself constitutes an aim of existence, that so-called well or ill-faring of these or those isolated individuals cannot be regarded as an essential element in the rational order of the universe. With more justice than happiness,—or a fortunate environment for individuals,—it is demanded of the grand aim of the world's existence, that it should foster, nay involve the execution and ratification of good, moral, righteous purposes. What makes men morally discontented (a discontent, by the by, on which they somewhat pride themselves), is that they do not find the present adapted to the realization of aims which they hold to be right and just (more especially in modern times, ideals of political constitutions); they contrast unfavourably things as they *are*, with their idea of things as they *ought* to be. In this case it is not private interest nor passion that desires gratification, but reason, justice, liberty; and equipped with this title, the demand in question assumes a lofty bearing, and readily adopts a position not merely of discontent, but of open revolt against the actual condition of the world. To estimate such a feeling and such views aright, the demands insisted upon, and the very dogmatic opinions asserted, must be examined. At no time so much as in our own, have such general principles and notions been advanced, or with greater assurance. If in days gone by, history seems to present itself as a struggle of passions; in our time—though displays of passion are not wanting —it exhibits partly a predominance of the struggle of notions assuming the authority of principles; partly that of passions and interests essentially subjective, but under the mask of such higher sanctions. The pretensions thus contended for as legitimate in the name of that which has been stated as the ultimate aim of Reason, pass accordingly, for absolute aims,—to the same extent as religion, morals, ethics. Nothing, as before remarked, is now more common than the complaint that the *ideals* which imagination sets up are not realised—that these glorious dreams are destroyed by cold actuality. These ideals—which in the voyage of life founder on the rocks of hard reality—may be in the first instance only subjective, and belong to the idiosyncrasy of the individual, imagining himself the highest and wisest. Such do not properly belong to this category. For the fancies which the individual in his isolation indulges, cannot be the model for universal reality; just as *universal* law is not designed for the units of the mass. These as such may, in fact, find their interests decidedly thrust into the background. But by the term "Ideal," we also understand the ideal of reason, of the good, of the true. Poets, as *e.g.* Schiller, have painted such ideals touchingly and with strong emotion, and with the deeply melancholy conviction that they could not be realised. In affirming, on the contrary that the universal Reason *does* realise itself, we have indeed nothing to do with the individual empirically regarded. That admits of degrees of better and worse, since here chance and particularity have received authority from the Idea to exercise their monstrous power. Much, therefore, in particular aspects of the grand phenomenon might be found fault with. This subjective fault-finding,—which, however, only keeps in view the individual and its deficiency, without taking notice of Reason pervading the whole,—is easy; and inasmuch as it asserts an excellent intention with regard to the good of the whole, and seems to result from a kindly heart, it feels authorized to give itself airs and assume great consequence. It is easier to discover a deficiency in individuals, in states, and in providence, than to see their real import and value.

For in this merely negative fault-finding a proud position is taken,
—one which overlooks the object, without having entered into it,—
without having comprehended its positive aspect. Age generally
makes men more tolerant; youth is always discontented. The toler-
ance of age is the result of the ripeness of a judgment which, not
merely as the result of indifference, is satisfied even with what is
inferior; but, more deeply taught by the grave experience of life,
has been led to perceive the substantial, solid worth of the object
in question. The insight then to which—in contradistinction from
those ideals—philosophy is to lead us, is, that the actual world is
as it ought to be—that the truly good—the universal divine reason
—is not a mere abstraction, but a vital principle capable of realising itself. This *good*, this *Reason*, in its most concrete form, is
God. God governs the world; the actual working of his government—the carrying out of his plan—is the history of the world.
This plan philosophy strives to comprehend; for only that which
has been developed as the result of it, possesses *bonâ fide* reality.
That which does not accord with it, is negative, worthless existence. Before the pure light of this divine Idea—which is no mere
ideal—the phantom of a world whose events are an incoherent
concourse of fortuitous circumstances, utterly vanishes. Philosophy
wishes to discover the substantial purport, the actual side of the
divine idea, and to justify the so much despised actuality of things;
for Reason is the comprehension of the divine work. But as to
what concerns the perversion, corruption, and ruin of religious,
ethical and moral purposes, and states of society generally, it must
be affirmed, that in their *essence* these are infinite and eternal;
but that the forms they assume may be of a limited order, and consequently belong to the domain of mere nature, and be subject
to the sway of chance. They are therefore perishable, and exposed
to decay and corruption. Religion and morality—in the same way
as inherently universal essences—have the peculiarity of being
present in the individual soul, in the full extent of their Idea, and
therefore truly and really; although they may not manifest themselves in it *in extenso,* and are not applied to fully developed relations. The religion, the morality of a limited sphere of life—that
of a shepherd or a peasant, *e.g.*—in its intensive concentration and
limitation to a few perfectly simple relations of life,—has infinite
worth; the same worth as the religion and morality of extensive

knowledge, and of an existence rich in the compass of its relations and actions. This inner focus—this simple region of the claims of subjective freedom,—the home of volition, resolution, and action, —the abstract sphere of conscience,—that which comprises the responsibility and moral value of the individual, remains untouched; and is quite shut out from the noisy din of the world's history— including not merely external and temporal changes, but also those entailed by the absolute necessity inseparable from the realization of the Idea of freedom itself. But as a general truth this must be regarded as settled, that whatever in the world possesses claims as noble and glorious, has nevertheless a higher existence above it. The claim of the world-spirit rises above all special claims.

These observations may suffice in reference to the means which the world-spirit uses for realising its Idea. Stated simply and abstractly, this mediation involves the activity of personal existences in whom Reason is present as their absolute, substantial being; but a basis, in the first instance, still obscure and unknown to them. But the subject becomes more complicated and difficult when we regard individuals not merely in their aspect of activity, but more concretely, in conjunction with a particular manifestation of that activity in their religion and morality,—forms of existence which are intimately connected with Reason, and share in its absolute claims. Here the relation of mere means to an end disappears, and the chief bearings of this seeming difficulty in reference to the absolute aim of Spirit, have been briefly considered.

31 The third point to be analysed is, therefore—what is the object to be realised by these means; *i.e.* what is the form it assumes in the realm of the actual. We have spoken of *means;* but in the carrying out of a subjective, limited aim, we have also to take into consideration the element of a *material,* either already present or which has to be procured. Thus the question would arise: What is the material in which the ideal of Reason is wrought out? The primary answer would be,—personality itself—human desires—subjectivity generally. In human knowledge and volition, as its material element, Reason attains positive existence. We have considered subjective volition where it has an object which is the truth and essence of a reality, viz. where it constitutes a great world-historical

passion. As a subjective will, occupied with limited passions, it is dependent, and can gratify its desires only within the limits of this dependence. But the subjective will has also a substantial life—a reality,—in which it moves in the region of *essential* being and has the essential itself as the object of its existence. This essential being is the union of the *subjective* with the *rational* will: it is the moral whole, the state, which is that form of actuality in which the individual has and enjoys his freedom; but on the condition of his recognition, believing in and willing that which is common to the whole. And this must not be understood as if the subjective will of the social unit attained its gratification and enjoyment through that common Will; as if this were a means provided for its benefit; as if the individual, in his relations to other individuals, thus limited his freedom, in order that this universal limitation— the mutual constraint of all—might secure a small space of liberty for each. Rather, we affirm, are law, morality, government, and they alone, the positive fact and completion of freedom. Freedom of a low and limited order, is mere caprice; which finds its exercise in the sphere of particular and limited desires.

Subjective volition—passion—is that which sets men in activity, that which effects "practical" actualization. The Idea is the inner spring of action; the state is the actually existing, realised moral life. For it is the unity of the universal, essential will, with that of the individual; and this is "morality." The individual living in this unity has a moral life; possesses a value that consists in this substantiality alone. Sophocles in his Antigone, says, "The divine commands are not of yesterday, nor of today; no, they have an infinite existence, and no one could say whence they came." The laws of morality are not accidental, but are the essentially rational. It is the very object of the state that what is essential in the practical activity of men, and in their dispositions, should be duly recognised; that it should have a manifest existence, and maintain its position. It is the absolute interest of Reason that this moral whole should exist; and herein lies the justification and merit of heroes who have founded states,—however rude these may have been. In the history of the world, only those peoples can come under our notice which form a state. For it must be understood that this latter is the realization of freedom, *i.e.* of the absolute final aim, and that it exists for its own sake. It must further

be understood that all the worth which the human being possesses
—all spiritual actuality, he possesses only through the state. For his
spiritual actuality consists in this, that his own essence—Reason—
is objectively present to him, that it possesses objective immediate
existence for him. Thus only is he fully conscious; thus only is he
a partaker of morality—of a just and moral social and political life.
For truth is the unity of the universal and subjective will; and the
universal is to be found in the state, in its laws, its universal and
rational arrangements. The state is the divine Idea as it exists on
earth. We have in it, therefore, the object of history in a more
definite shape than before; that in which freedom obtains objectivity, and lives in the enjoyment of this objectivity. For law is the
objectivity of spirit; volition in its true form. Only that will which
obeys law, is free; for it obeys itself—it is independent and so free.
When the state or our country constitutes a community of existence; when the subjective will of man submits to laws,—the contradiction between liberty and necessity vanishes. The rational
has necessary existence, as being the reality and substance of
things, and we are free in recognising it as law, and following
it as the substance of our own being. The objective and the
subjective will are then reconciled, and present one identical ho-
mogeneous whole. For the morality (Sittlichkeit) of the state is not
of that ethical (moralische) reflective kind, in which one's own
conviction bears sway; this latter is rather the peculiarity of the
modern time, while the true antique morality is based on the principle of abiding by one's duty [to the state at large]. An Athenian
citizen did what was required of him, as it were from instinct; but
if I reflect on the object of my activity, I must have the consciousness that my will has been called into exercise. But morality is
duty—substantial right—a "*second* nature" as it has been justly
called; for the *first* nature of man is his primary merely animal
existence.

The development *in extenso* of the Idea of the state belongs to
the philosophy of jurisprudence; but it must be observed that in
the theories of our time various errors are current respecting it,
which pass for established truths, and have become fixed preju-
dices. We will mention only a few of them, giving prominence to
such as have a reference to the object of our history.

The error which first meets us is the direct contradictory of our principle that the state presents the realization of freedom; the opinion, viz., that man is free by *nature,* but that in *society,* in the state—to which nevertheless he is irresistibly impelled—he must limit this natural freedom. That man is free by nature is quite correct in one sense; viz., that he is so according to the idea of humanity; but we imply thereby that he is such only in virtue of his destiny—that he has an undeveloped power to become such; for the "nature" of an object is exactly synonymous with its "Idea." But the view in question imports more than this. When man is spoken of as "free by nature," the mode of his existence as well as his destiny is implied. His merely natural and primary condition is intended. In this sense a "state of nature" is assumed in which mankind at large are in the possession of their natural rights with the unconstrained exercise and enjoyment of their freedom. This assumption is not indeed raised to the dignity of the historical fact; it would indeed be difficult, were the attempt seriously made, to point out any such condition as actually existing, or as having ever occurred. Examples of a savage state of life can be pointed out, but they are marked by brutal passions and deeds of violence; while, however rude and simple their conditions, they involve social arrangements which (to use the common phrase) *restrain* freedom. That assumption is one of those nebulous images which theory produces; an idea which it cannot avoid originating, but which it fathers upon real existence, without sufficient historical justification.

What we find such a state of nature to be in actual experience, answers exactly to the idea of a *merely* natural condition. Freedom as the *ideal* of that which is original and natural, does not exist *as original and natural.* Rather must it be first sought out and won; and that by an incalculable medial discipline of the intellectual and moral powers. The state of nature is, therefore, predominantly that of injustice and violence, of untamed natural impulses, of inhuman deeds and feelings. Limitation is certainly produced by society and the state, but it is a limitation of the mere brute emotions and rude instincts; as also, in a more advanced stage of culture, of the premeditated self-will of caprice and passion. This kind of constraint is part of the instrumentality by which only, the consciousness of freedom and the desire for its attainment, in its true—that is rational and ideal form—can be

obtained. To the notion of freedom, law and morality are in-
dispensably requisite; and they are in and for themselves, universal existences, objects and aims; which are discovered only by
the activity of thought, separating itself from the merely sensuous,
and developing itself, in opposition thereto; and which must on
the other hand, be introduced into and incorporated with the
originally sensuous will, and that contrarily to its natural inclination. The perpetually recurring misapprehension of freedom consists in regarding that term only in its *formal*, subjective sense,
abstracted from its essential objects and aims; thus a constraint
put upon impulse, desire, passion—pertaining to the particular
individual as such—a limitation of caprice and self-will is regarded
as a fettering of freedom. We should on the contrary look upon
such limitation as the indispensable proviso of emancipation.
Society and the state are the very conditions in which freedom is
realised.

We must notice a second view, contravening the principle of
the development of moral relations into a legal form. The *patriarchal* condition is regarded—either in reference to the entire
race of man, or to some branches of it—as exclusively that condition of things, in which the legal element is combined with a
due recognition of the moral and emotional parts of our nature;
and in which justice as united with these, truly and really influences the intercourse of the social units. The basis of the patriarchal condition is the family relation; which develops the
primary form of conscious morality, succeeded by that of the state
as its *second* phase. The patriarchal condition is one of transition,
in which the family has already advanced to the position of a race
or people; where the union, therefore, has already ceased to be
simply a bond of love and confidence, and has become one of
plighted service. We must first examine the ethical principle of the
family. The family may be reckoned as virtually a single person;
since its members have either mutually surrendered their individual personality, (and consequently their legal position towards
each other, with the rest of their particular interests and desires)
as in the case of the parents; or have not yet attained such an
independent personality,—(the children,—who are primarily in
that merely natural condition already mentioned). They live,
therefore, in a unity of feeling, love, confidence, and faith in each

other. And in a relation of mutual love, the one individual has the consciousness of himself in the consciousness of the other; he lives out of self; and in this mutual self-renunciation each regains the life that had been virtually transferred to the other; gains, in fact, that other's existence and his own, as involved with that other. The further interests connected with the necessities and external concerns of life, as well as the development that has to take place within their circle, *i.e.* of the children, constitute a common object for the members of the family. The spirit of the family—the Penates—form one substantial being, as much as the spirit of a people in the state; and morality in both cases consists in a feeling, a consciousness, and a will, not limited to individual personality and interest, but embracing the common interests of the members generally. But this unity is in the case of the family essentially one of *feeling;* not advancing beyond the limits of the merely *natural.* The piety of the family relation should be respected in the highest degree by the state; by its means the state obtains as its members individuals who are already moral (for as mere *persons* they are not) and who in uniting to form a state bring with them that sound basis of a political edifice—the capacity of feeling one with a whole. But the expansion of the family to a patriarchal unity carries us beyond the ties of blood-relationship—the simply natural elements of that basis; and outside of these limits the members of the community must enter upon the position of independent personality. A review of the patriarchal condition, *in extenso,* would lead us to give special attention to the theocratical constitution. The head of the patriarchal clan is also its priest. If the family in its general relations, is not yet separated from civic society and the state, the separation of religion from it has also not yet taken place; and so much the less since the piety of the hearth is itself a profoundly subjective state of feeling.

We have considered two aspects of freedom,—the objective and the subjective; if, therefore, freedom is asserted to consist in the individuals of a state all agreeing in its arrangements, it is evident that only the subjective aspect is regarded. The natural inference from this principle is, that no law can be valid without the approval of all. This difficulty is attempted to be obviated by the decision that the minority must yield to the majority; the majority therefore bear the sway. But long ago J. J. Rousseau remarked, that in that case there would be no longer freedom, for the will of the *minority* would cease to be respected. At the Polish Diet each single member had to give his consent before any political step could be taken; and this kind of freedom it was that ruined the state. Besides, it is a dangerous and false prejudice, that the people *alone* have reason and insight, and know what justice is; for each popular faction may represent itself as the people, and the question as to what constitutes the state is one of advanced science, and not of popular decision.

If the principle of regard for the individual will is recognised as the only basis of political liberty, viz., that nothing should be done by or for the state to which all the members of the body politic have not given their sanction, we have, properly speaking, no *constitution*. The only arrangement that would be necessary, would be, first, a centre having no *will* of its own, but which should take into consideration what appeared to be the necessities of the state; and, secondly, a contrivance for calling the members of the state together, for taking the votes, and for performing the arithmetical operations of reckoning and comparing the number of votes for the different propositions, and thereby deciding upon them. The state is an *abstraction*, having its generic existence in its citizens; but it is an actuality, and its simply generic existence must embody itself in individual will and activity. The want of government and political administration in general is felt; this necessitates the selection and separation from the rest of those who have to take the helm in political affairs, to decide concerning them, and to give orders to other citizens, with a view to the execution of their plans. If, *e. g.,* even the people in a democracy resolve on a war, a general must head the army. It is only by a constitution that the *abstraction*—the state—attains life and actuality; but this involves the distinction between those who command and those who obey.—Yet obedience seems inconsistent with liberty, and those who command appear to do the very opposite of that which the fundamental notion of the state, viz., that of freedom, requires. It is, however, urged that,—though the distinction between commanding and obeying is absolutely necessary, because affairs could not go on without it—and indeed this seems only a compulsory limitation, external to and even contravening freedom in the abstract—the constitution should be at least so framed, that the citizens may obey as little as possible, and the smallest modicum of free volition be left to the commands of the superiors;—that the substance of that for which subordination is necessary, even in its most important bearings, should be decided and resolved on by the people—by the will of many or of all the citizens; though it is supposed to be thereby provided that the state should be possessed of vigour and strength as an actuality—an individual unity.—The primary consideration is, then, the distinction between the governing and the governed, and political constitutions in the abstract have been rightly divided into monarchy, aristocracy, and democracy; which gives occasion, however, to the remark that monarchy itself must be further divided into despotism and monarchy proper; that in all the divisions to which the leading notion gives rise, only the generic character is to be made prominent,—it being not intended thereby that the particular category under review should be exhausted as a form, order, or kind in its *concrete* development. But especially it must be observed, that the above-mentioned divisions admit of a multitude of particular modifications,—not only such as lie within the limits of those classes themselves,—but also such as are mixtures of several of these essentially distinct classes, and which are consequently misshapen, unstable, and inconsistent forms. In such a collision, the concerning question is, what is the *best constitution;* that is, by what arrangement, organization, or mechanism of the power of the state its object can be most surely attained. This object may indeed be variously understood; for instance, as the calm enjoyment of life on the part of the citizens, or as universal happiness. Such aims have suggested the so-called ideals of constitution, and,—as a particular branch of the subject,—ideals of the education of princes (Fenelon), or of the governing body—the aristocracy at large (Plato); for the chief point they treat of is the condition of those subjects who stand at the head of affairs; and in these ideals the concrete details of political organization are not at all considered. The inquiry into the best constitution is frequently treated as if not only the theory were an affair of subjective independent conviction, but as if the introduction of a constitution recognised as the best,—or as superior to others,—could be the result of a resolve adopted in this theoretical manner; as if the form of a constitution were a matter of free choice.

determined by nothing else but reflection. Of this artless fashion
was that deliberation,—not indeed of the Persian *people,* but of the
Persian *grandees,* who had conspired to overthrow the pseudo-
Smerdis and the Magi, after their undertaking had succeeded,
and when there was no scion of the royal family living,—as to what
constitution they should introduce into Persia; and Herodotus
gives an equally naïve account of this deliberation.

In the present day, the constitution of a country and people is
not represented as so entirely dependent on free and deliberate
choice. The fundamental but abstractly (and therefore imper-
fectly) entertained conception of freedom, has resulted in the re-
public being very generally regarded—in *theory*—as the only just
and true political constitution. Many even, who occupy elevated
official positions under monarchical constitutions—so far from
being opposed to this idea—are actually its supporters; only they
see that such a constitution, though the best, cannot be realised
under all circumstances; and that—while men are what they are—
we must be satisfied with less freedom; the monarchical constitution—under the given circumstances, and the present moral condition of the people—being even regarded as the most advantageous.
In this view also, the necessity of a particular constitution is made
to depend on the condition of the people in such a way as if the
latter were non-essential and accidental. This representation is
founded on the distinction which the reflective understanding
makes between a notion and the corresponding reality: holding
to an abstract and consequently untrue notion; not grasping it in
its completeness, or—which is virtually, though not in point of
form, the same—not taking a concrete view of a people and a state.
We shall have to shew further on, that the constitution adopted
by a people makes one substance—one spirit—with its religion, its
art and philosophy, or, at least, with its conceptions and thoughts
—its culture generally; not to expatiate upon the additional influences, *ab extrâ,* of climate, of neighbours, of its place in the
world. A state is an individual totality, of which you cannot select
any particular side, although a supremely important one, such as
its political constitution; and deliberate and decide respecting it in
that isolated form. Not only is that constitution most intimately
connected with and dependent on those other spiritual forces; but
the form of the entire moral and intellectual individuality—com-

prising all the forces it embodies—is only a step in the development of the grand whole,—with its place preappointed in the process; a fact which gives the highest sanction to the constitution in question, and establishes its absolute necessity.—The origin of a state involves imperious lordship on the one hand, instinctive submission on the other. But even obedience—lordly power, and the fear inspired by a ruler—in itself implies some degree of voluntary connection. Even in barbarous states this is the case; it is not the isolated will of individuals that prevails; individual pretensions are relinquished, and the general will is the essential bond of political union. This unity of the general and the particular is the Idea itself, manifesting itself as a *state,* and which subsequently undergoes further development within itself. The abstract yet necessitated process in the development of truly independent states is as follows:—They begin with regal power, whether of patriarchal or military origin. In the next phase, particularity and individuality assert themselves in the form of aristocracy and democracy. Lastly, we have the subjection of these separate interests to a single power; but which can be absolutely none other than one outside of which those spheres have an independent position, viz., the monarchical. Two phases of royalty, therefore, must be distinguished,—a primary and a secondary one. This process is necessitated, so that the form of government assigned to a particular stage of development *must* present itself: it is therefore no matter of choice, but is that form which is adapted to the spirit of the people.

In a constitution the main feature of interest is the self-development of the *rational,* that is, the *political* condition of a people; the setting free of the successive elements of the Idea: so that the several powers in the state manifest themselves as separate,—attain their appropriate and special perfection,—and yet in this independent condition, work together for one object, and are held together by it—*i.e.,* form an organic whole. The state is thus the embodiment of rational freedom, realizing and recognizing itself in an objectivity form. For its objective consists in this,—that its successive stages are not merely ideal, but are present in an appropriate reality; and that in their separate and several working, they are absolutely merged in that agency by which the totality—

the soul—the individual unity—is produced, and of which it is the result.

The state is the idea of Spirit in the external manifestation of human will and its freedom. It is to the state, therefore, that change in the aspect of history indissolubly attaches itself; and the successive phases of the Idea manifest themselves in it as distinct political *principles*. The constitutions under which world-historical peoples have reached their culmination, are peculiar to them; and therefore do not present a generally applicable political basis. Were it otherwise, the differences of similar constitutions would consist only in a peculiar method of expanding and developing that generic basis; whereas they really originate in diversity of principle. From the comparison therefore of the political institutions of the ancient world-historical peoples, it so happens, that for the most recent principle of a constitution—for the principle of our own times—nothing (so to speak) can be learned. In science and art it is quite otherwise; *e. g.,* the ancient philosophy is so decidedly the basis of the modern, that it is inevitably contained in the latter, and constitutes its basis. In this case the relation is that of a continuous development of the same structure, whose foundation-stone, walls, and roof have remained what they were. In art, the Greek itself, in its original form, furnishes us the best models. But in regard to political constitution, it is quite otherwise: here the ancient and the modern have not their essential principle in common. Abstract definitions and dogmas respecting just government,—importing that intelligence and virtue ought to bear sway—are, indeed, common to both. But nothing is so absurd as to look to Greeks, Romans, or Orientals, for models for the political arrangements of our time. From the East may be derived beautiful pictures of a patriarchal condition, of paternal government, and of devotion to it on the part of peoples; from Greeks and Romans, descriptions of popular liberty. Among the latter we find the idea of a free constitution admitting all the citizens to a share in deliberations and resolves respecting the affairs and laws of the commonwealth. In our times, too, this is its general acceptation; only with this modification, that—since our states are so large, and there are so many of "the many," the latter,—direct action being impossible,—should by the indirect method of elective substitution express their concurrence with resolves affecting the common weal; that is, that for legislative purposes generally, the people should be represented by deputies. The so-called representative constitution is that form of government with which we connect the idea of a free constitution, and this notion has become a rooted prejudice. On this theory people and government are separated. But there is a perversity in this antithesis; an ill-intentioned *ruse* designed to insinuate that the people are the totality of the state. Besides, the basis of this view is the principle of isolated individuality—the absolute validity of the subjective will—a dogma which we have already investigated. The great point is, that freedom in its ideal conception has not subjective will and caprice for its principle, but the recognition of the universal will; and that the process by which freedom is realised is the free development of its successive stages. The subjective will is a merely formal determination—*a carte blanche*—not including what it is that is willed. Only the *rational* will is that universal principle which independently determines and unfolds its own being, and develops its successive elemental phases as organic members. Of this Gothic-cathedral architecture the ancients knew nothing.

At an earlier stage of the discussion, we established the two elemental considerations: first, the *idea* of freedom as the absolute and final aim; secondly, the *means* for realising it, *i. e.* the subjective side of knowledge and will. with its life, movement, and activity. We then recognised the state as the moral whole and the reality of freedom, and consequently as the objective unity of these two elements. For although we make this distinction into two aspects for our consideration, it must be remarked that they are intimately connected; and that their connection is involved in the idea of each when examined separately. We have, on the one hand, recognised the Idea in the definite form of freedom conscious of and willing itself,—having itself alone as its object: involving at the same time, the pure and simple idea of Reason, and likewise, that which we have called subject—self-consciousness—Spirit actually existing in the world. If, on the other hand, we consider subjectivity, we find that subjective knowledge and will is thought. But by the very act of thoughtful cognition and volition, I will the universal object—the substance of absolute Reason. We observe, therefore, an essential union between the objective side—the

Idea,—and the subjective side—the personality that conceives and wills it.—The *objective* existence of this union is the state, which is therefore the basis and centre of the other concrete elements of the life of a people,—of art, of law, of morals, of religion, of science. All the activity of Spirit has only this object—the becoming conscious of this union, *i.e.,* of its own freedom. Among the forms of this conscious union *religion* occupies the highest position. In it, Spirit—rising above the limitations of temporal and secular existence—becomes conscious of the Absolute Spirit, and in this consciousness of the self-existent Being, renounces its individual interest; it lays this aside in devotion—a state of mind in which it refuses to occupy itself any longer with the limited and particular. By sacrifice man expresses his renunciation of his property, his will, his individual feelings. The religious concentration of the soul appears in the form of feeling; it nevertheless passes also into reflection; a form of worship (*cultus*) is a result of reflection. The second form of the union of the objective and subjective in the human spirit is art. This advances farther into the realm of the actual and sensuous than religion. In its noblest walk it is occupied with representing, not indeed, the spirit of God, but certainly the form of God; and in its secondary aims, that which is divine and spiritual generally. Its office is to render visible the divine; presenting it to the imaginative and intuitive faculty. But the true is the object not only of conception and feeling, as in religion,—and of intuition, as in art,—but also of the thinking faculty; and this gives us the third form of the union in question—*philosophy*. This is consequently the highest, freest, and wisest phase. Of course we are not intending to investigate these three phases here; they have only suggested themselves in virtue of their occupying the same general ground as the object here considered —the state.

The general principle which manifests itself and becomes an object of consciousness in the state,—the form under which all that the state includes is brought,—is the whole of that cycle of phenomena which constitutes the *culture* of a nation. But the definite *substance* that receives the form of universality, and exists in that concrete actuality which is the state,—is the spirit of the people itself. The actual state is animated by this spirit, in all its particular affairs—its wars, institutions, &c. But man must also attain a conscious realization of this his Spirit and essential nature, and of his original identity with it. For we said that moralty is the identity of the *subjective* or *personal* with the *universal* will. Now the mind must give itself an express consciousness of this; and the focus of this knowledge is *religion*. Art and science are only various aspects and forms of the same substantial being. In considering religion, the chief point of enquiry is, whether it recognises the true—the Idea—only in its separate, abstract form, or in its true unity; in *separation*—God being represented in an abstract form as the highest being, lord of heaven and earth, living in a remote region far from human actualities,—or in its *unity*,—God, as unity of the universal and individual; the individual itself assuming the aspect of positive and real existence in the idea of the incarnation. Religion is the sphere in which a nation gives itself the definition of that which it regards as the true. A definition contains everything that belongs to the essence of an object; reducing its nature to its simple characteristic predicate, as a mirror for every predicate,—the generic soul pervading all its details. The conception of God, therefore, constitutes the general basis of a people's character.

In this aspect, religion stands in the closest connection with the political principle. Freedom can exist only where individuality is recognised as having its positive and real existence in the divine being. The connection may be further explained thus:—secular existence, as merely temporal—occupied with particular interests— is consequently only relative and unauthorized; and receives its validity only in as far as the universal soul that pervades it—its principle—receives absolute validity; which it cannot have unless it is recognised as the definite manifestation, the phenomenal existence of the divine essence. On this account it is that the state rests on religion. We hear this often repeated in our times, though for the most part nothing further is meant than that individual subjects as God-fearing men would be more disposed and ready to perform their duty; since obedience to king and law so naturally follows in the train of reverence for God. This reverence, indeed, since it exalts the general over the special, may even turn upon the latter,—become fanatical,—and work with incendiary and destructive violence against the state, its institutions, and arrangements. Religious feeling, therefore, it is thought, should be sober—kept

in a certain degree of coolness,—that it may not storm against and
bear down that which should be defended and preserved by it.
The possibility of such a catastrophe is at least latent in it.

While, however, the correct sentiment is adopted, that the state
is based on religion, the position thus assigned to religion supposes the state already to exist; and that subsequently, in order
to maintain it, religion must be brought into it—in buckets and
bushels as it were—and impressed upon people's hearts. It is quite
true that men must be trained to religion, but not as to something
whose existence has yet to begin. For in affirming that the state is
based on religion—that it has its roots in it—we virtually assert that
the former has proceeded from the latter; and that this derivation
is going on now and will always continue; i. e., the principles of
the state must be regarded as valid in and for themselves, which
can only be in so far as they are recognised as determinate manifestations of the divine nature. The form of religion, therefore,
decides that of the state and its constitution. The latter actually
originated in the particular religion adopted by the nation; so that,
in fact, the Athenian or the Roman state was possible only in
connection with the specific form of heathenism existing among
the respective peoples; just as a Catholic state has a spirit and
constitution different from that of a Protestant one.

If that outcry—that urging and striving for the implantation of
religion in the community—were an utterance of anguish and a
call for help, as it often seems to be, expressing the danger of religion having vanished, or being about to vanish entirely from the
state,—that would be fearful indeed,—worse, in fact, than this outcry supposes; for it implies the belief in a resource against the
evil, viz., the implantation and inculcation of religion; whereas
religion is by no means a thing to be so produced; its *self-production* (and there can be no other) lies much deeper.

Another and opposite folly which we meet with in our time, is
that of pretending to invent and carry out political constitutions
independently of religion. The Catholic confession, although
sharing the Christian name with the Protestant, does not concede
to the state an inherent justice and morality,—a concession which
in the Protestant principle is fundamental. This tearing away of
the political morality of the constitution from its natural connection, is necessary to the genius of that religion, inasmuch as it does

not recognise justice and morality as independent and substantial. But thus excluded from intrinsic worth,—torn away from their last refuge—the sanctuary of conscience—the calm retreat where religion has its abode,—the principles and institutions of political legislation are destitute of a real centre, to the same degree as they are compelled to remain abstract and indefinite.

Summing up what has been said of the state, we find that we have been led to call its vital principle, as actuating the individuals who compose it,—morality. The state, its laws, its arrangements, constitute the rights of its members; its natural features, its mountains, air, and waters, are *their* country, their fatherland, their outward material property; the history of this state, *their* deeds; what their ancestors have produced, belongs to them and lives in their memory. All is their possession, just as they are possessed by it; for it constitutes their existence, their being.

Their imagination is occupied with the ideas thus presented, while the adoption of these laws, and of a fatherland so conditioned is the expression of their will. It is this matured totality which thus constitutes *one* being, the spirit of *one* people. To it the individual members belong; each unit is the son of his nation, and at the same time—in as far as the state to which he belongs is undergoing development—the son of his age. None remains behind it, still less advances beyond it. This spiritual being (the spirit of his time) is his; he is a representative of it; it is that in which he originated, and in which he lives. Among the Athenians the word Athens had a double import; suggesting primarily, a complex of political institutions, but no less, in the second place, that goddess who represented the spirit of the people and its unity.

This spirit of a people is a *determinate* and particular spirit, and is, as just stated, further modified by the degree of its historical development. This spirit, then, constitutes the basis and substance of those other forms of a nation's consciousness, which have been noticed. For Spirit in its self-consciousness must become an object of contemplation to itself, and objectivity involves, in the first instance, the rise of differences which make up a total of distinct spheres of objective spirit; in the same way as the soul exists only as the complex of its faculties, which in their form of concentration in a simple unity produce that soul. It is thus *One In-*

dividuality which, presented in its essence as God, is honoured and enjoyed in *religion;* which is exhibited as an object of sensuous contemplation in *art;* and is apprehended as an intellectual conception, in *philosophy.* In virtue of the original identity of their essence, purport, and object, these various forms are inseparably united with the spirit of the state. Only in connection with this particular religion, can this particular political constitution exist; just as in such or such a state, such or such a philosophy or order of art.

The remark next in order is, that each particular national genius is to be treated as only one individual in the process of universal history. For that history is the exhibition of the divine, absolute development of Spirit in its highest forms,—that gradation by which it attains its truth and consciousness of itself. The forms which these grades of progress assume are the characteristic "national spirits" of history; the peculiar tenor of their moral life, of their government, their art, religion, and science. To realise these grades is the boundless impulse of the World-Spirit—the goal of its irresistible urging; for this division into organic members, and the full development of each, is its Idea.—Universal history is exclusively occupied with shewing how Spirit comes to a recognition and adoption of the truth: the dawn of knowledge appears; it begins to discover salient principles, and at last it arrives at full consciousness.

Having, therefore, learned the abstract characteristics of the nature of Spirit, the means which it uses to realize its Idea, and the shape assumed by it in its complete realisation in phenomenal existence—namely, the state—nothing further remains for this introductory section to contemplate but the course of the world's history.

The mutations which history presents have been long characterised in the general, as an advance to something better, more perfect. The changes that take place in nature—how infinitely manifold soever they may be—exhibit only a perpetually self-repeating cycle; in nature there happens "nothing new under the sun," and the multiform play of its phenomena so far induces a feeling of *ennui;* only in those changes which take place in the region of Spirit does anything new arise. This peculiarity in the world of mind has indicated in the case of man an altogether different destiny from that of merely natural objects—in which we find always one and the same stable character, to which all change reverts;—namely, a *real* capacity for change, and that for the better, —an impulse of *perfectibility*. This principle, which reduces change itself under a law, has met with an unfavorable reception from religions—such as the Catholic—and from states claiming as their just right a stereotyped, or at least a stable position. If the mutability of worldly things in general—political constitutions, for instance—is conceded, either religion (as the religion of *truth*) is absolutely excepted, or the difficulty escaped by ascribing changes, revolutions, and abrogations of immaculate theories and institutions, to accidents or imprudence,—but principally to the levity and evil passions of man. The principle of perfectibility indeed is almost as indefinite a term as mutability in general; it is without scope or goal, and has no standard by which to estimate the changes in question: the improved, more perfect, state of things towards which it professedly tends is altogether undetermined.

The principle of *development* involves also the existence of a latent germ of being—a capacity or potentiality striving to actualize itself. This formal conception finds actual existence in Spirit; which has the history of the world for its theatre, its possession, and the sphere of its actualization. It is not of such a nature as to be tossed to and fro amid the superficial play of accidents, but is rather the absolute arbiter of things; entirely unmoved by contingencies, which, indeed, it applies and manages for its own purposes. Development, however, is also a property of organized natural objects. Their existence presents itself, not as an exclusively dependent one, subjected to external changes, but as one which expands itself in virtue of an external unchangeable principle; a simple essence,—whose existence, *i. e.*, as a germ, is primarily simple,—but which subsequently develops a variety of parts, that become involved with other objects, and consequently live through a continuous process of changes;—a process nevertheless, that results in the very contrary of change, and is even transformed into a *vis conservatrix* of the organic principle, and the form embodying it. Thus the organized *individuum* produces itself; it expands itself *actually* to what it was always *potentially*. So Spirit is only that which it attains by its own efforts; it makes itself *actually* what it always was *potentially*.—That development (of *natural organisms*) takes place in a direct, unopposed, unhindered manner. Between the notion and its actualization—the essential constitution of the original germ and the conformity to it of the existence derived from it—no disturbing influence can intrude. But in relation to Spirit it is quite otherwise. The actualization of *its* idea is mediated by consciousness and will; these very faculties are, in the first instance, sunk in their primary *merely* natural life; the first object and goal of their striving is the realisation of their merely natural destiny,—but which, since it is Spirit that animates it, is possessed of vast attractions and displays great power and [moral] richness. Thus Spirit is at war with itself; it has to overcome itself as its most formidable obstacle. That development which in the sphere of nature is a peaceful growth, is in that of Spirit, a severe, a mighty conflict with itself. What Spirit really strives for is the realisation of its ideal being; but in doing so, it hides that goal from its own vision, and is proud and well satisfied in this alienation from it.

Its expansion, therefore, does not present the harmless tranquillity of mere growth, as does that of organic life, but a stern reluctant working against itself. It exhibits, moreover, not the mere formal conception of development, but the attainment of a definite result. The goal of attainment we determined at the outset: it is Spirit in its *completeness*, in its essential nature, *i. e.*, freedom. This is the fundamental object, and therefore also the leading principle of the development,—that whereby it receives meaning and importance (as in the Roman history, Rome is the object—consequently that which directs our consideration of the facts related); as, conversely, the phenomena of the process have resulted from this principle alone, and only as referred to it, possess a sense and value. There are many considerable periods in history in which this development seems to have been intermitted; in which, we might rather say, the whole enormous gain of previous culture appears to have been entirely lost; after which, unhappily, a new commencement has been necessary, made in the hope of recovering—by the assistance of some remains saved from the wreck of a former civilization, and by dint of a renewed incalculable expenditure of strength and time,—one of the regions which had been an ancient possession of that civilization. We behold also *continued* processes of growth; structures and systems of culture in particular spheres, rich in kind, and well developed in every direction. The merely formal and indeterminate view of development in general can neither assign to one form of expansion superiority over the other, nor render comprehensible the object of that decay of older periods of growth; but must regard such occurrences,—or, to speak more particularly, the retrocessions they exhibit,—as external contingencies; and can only judge of particular modes of development from indeterminate points of view; which—since the development as such, is all in all—are relative and not absolute goals of attainment.

Universal history exhibits the *gradation* in the development of that principle whose substantial *purport* is the consciousness of freedom. The analysis of the successive grades, in their abstract form, belongs to logic; in their concrete aspect to the philosophy of spirit. Here it is sufficient to state that the first step in the process presents that immersion of Spirit in nature which has been already referred to; the second shows it as advancing to the consciousness of its freedom. But this initial separation from nature is imperfect and partial, since it is derived immediately from the merely natural state, is consequently related to it, and is still encumbered with it as an essentially connected element. The third step is the elevation of the soul from this still limited and special form of freedom to its pure universal form; that state in which the spiritual essence attains the consciousness and feeling of itself. These grades are the ground-principles of the general process; but how each of them on the other hand involves within *itself* a process of formation,—constituting the links in a dialectic of transition,—to particularise this may be reserved for the sequel.

Here we have only to indicate that Spirit begins with a germ of infinite possibility, but *only* possibility,—containing its substantial existence in an undeveloped form, as the object and goal which it reaches only in its resultant—full actuality. In actual existence progress appears as an advancing from the imperfect to the more perfect; but the former must not be understood abstractly as *only* the imperfect, but as something which involves the very opposite of itself—the so-called perfect as a *germ* or impulse. So—reflectively, at least—*possibility* points to something destined to become actual; the Aristotelian *dúnamis* is also *potentia,* power and might. Thus the imperfect, as involving its opposite, is a contradiction, which certainly exists, but which is continually annulled and solved; the instinctive movement—the inherent impulse in the life of the soul—to break through the rind of mere nature, sensuousness, and that which is alien to it, and to attain to the light of consciousness, *i. e.* to itself.

We have already made the remark how the commencement of the history of Spirit must be conceived so as to be in harmony with its idea—in its bearing on the representations that have been made of a primitive *"natural* condition,*"* in which freedom and justice are supposed to exist, or to have existed. This was, however, nothing more than an assumption of historical existence, conceived in the twilight of theorising reflection. A pretension of quite another order,—not a mere inference of reasoning, but making the claim of historical fact, and that supernaturally confirmed, —is put forth in connection with a different view that is now widely promulgated by a certain group. This view takes up the the idea of the primitive paradisical condition of man, which had been previously expanded by the theologians, after their fashion, —involving, *e.g.,* the supposition that God spoke with Adam in Hebrew,—but re-modelled to suit other requirements. The high authority appealed to in the first instance is the biblical narrative. But this depicts the primitive condition, partly only in the few well-known traits, but partly either as in man generically,—human nature at large,—or, so far as Adam is to be taken as an individual, and consequently one person,—as existing and completed in *this one,* or *only in one* human pair. The biblical account by no means justifies us in imagining a *people,* and an historical condition of such people, existing in that primitive form; still less does it warrant us in attributing to them the possession of a perfectly developed knowledge of God and nature. "Nature," so the fiction runs, "like a clear mirror of God's creation, had originally lain revealed and transparent to the unclouded eye of man."[1] Divine truth is imagined to have been equally manifest. It is even hinted, though left in some degree of obscurity, that in this primary condition men were in possession of an indefinitely extended and already expanded body of religious truths immediately revealed by

---

[1] Fr. von Schlegel, "Philosophy of History," p. 91, Bohn's Standard Library.

God. This theory affirms that all religions had their historical commencement in this primitive knowledge, and that they polluted and obscured the original truth by the monstrous creations of error and depravity; though in all the mythologies invented by error, traces of that origin and of those primitive true dogmas are supposed to be present and cognizable. An important interest, therefore, accrues to the investigation of the history of ancient peoples, that, viz., of the endeavour to trace their annals up to the point where such fragments of the primary revelation are to be met with in greater purity than lower down.[1]

We owe to the interest which has occasioned these investigations, very much that is valuable; but this investigation bears direct testimony against itself, for it would seem to be awaiting the issue of an historical demonstration of that which is presupposed by it as historically established. That advanced condition of the knowledge of God, and of other scientific, *e.g.*, astronomical knowledge (such as has been falsely attributed to the Hindoos); and the assertion that such a condition occurred at the very be-

[1] We have to thank this interest for many valuable discoveries in Oriental literature, and for a renewed study of treasures previously known, in the department of ancient Asiatic culture, mythology, religions, history. In those Catholic countries where a refined literary taste prevails, governments have yielded to the requirements of speculative inquiry, and have felt the necessity of allying themselves with learning and philosophy. Eloquently and impressively has the Abbé Lamennais reckoned it among the criteria of the true religion, that it must be the universal—that is, catholic—and the oldest in date; and the congregation has laboured zealously and diligently in France towards rendering such assertions no longer mere pulpit tirades and authoritative dicta, such as were deemed sufficient formerly. The religion of Buddha—a god man—which has prevailed to such an enormous extent, has especially attracted attention. The Indian Timûrtis, as also the Chinese abstraction of the trinity, has furnished clearer evidence in point of subject matter. The savants, M. Abel Remusat and M. Saint Martin, on the one hand, have undertaken the most meritorious investigations in the Chinese literature, with a view to make this also a base of operations for researches in the Mongolian and, if such were possible, in the Thibetian; on the other hand, Baron von Eckstein, in his way (*i.e.*, adopting from Germany superficial physical conceptions and mannerisms, in the style of Fr. v. Schlegel, though with more geniality than the latter) in his periodical, "Le Catholique,"—has furthered the cause of that primitive Catholicism generally, and in particular has gained for the savants of the congregation the support of the government; so that it has even set on foot expeditions to the East, in order to discover there treasures still concealed; (from which further disclosures have been anticipated, respecting profound theological questions, particularly on the higher antiquity and sources of Buddhism), and with a view to promote the interest of Catholicism by this circuitous but scientifically interesting method.

ginning of history,—or that the religions of various nations were traditionally derived from it, and have developed themselves in degeneracy and depravation (as is represented in the rudely-conceived so-called "emanation system,");—all these are suppositions which neither have, nor,—if we may contrast with their arbitrary subjective origin, the true conception of history,—can attain historical confirmation.

The only consistent and worthy method which philosophical investigation can adopt, is to take up history where rationality begins to manifest itself in the actual conduct of the world's affairs (not where it is merely an undeveloped potentiality),—where a condition of things is present in which it realises itself in consciousness, will and action. The inorganic existence of Spirit—that of abstract freedom—unconscious *torpidity* in respect to good and evil (and consequently to laws), or, if we please to term it so, "blessed ignorance,"—is itself not a subject of history. *Natural,* and at the same time *religious* morality, is the piety of the *family.* In this social relation, morality consists in the members behaving towards each other *not as individuals*—possessing an independent will; not as persons. The family therefore, is excluded from that process of development in which history takes its rise. But when this self-involved spiritual unity steps beyond this circle of feeling and natural love, and first attains the consciousness of personality, we have that dark, dull centre of indifference, in which neither nature nor Spirit is open and transparent; and for which nature and Spirit can become open and transparent only by means of a further process,—a very lengthened culture of that will at length become self-conscious. Consciousness alone is clearness; and is that alone for which God (or any other existence) can be revealed. In its true form,—in absolute universality—nothing can be manifested except to consciousness made percipient of it. Freedom is nothing but the recognition and adoption of such universal substantial objects as right and law, and the production of a reality that is accordant with them—the state. Nations may have passed a long life before arriving at this their destination, and during this period, they may have attained considerable culture in some directions. This ante-historical period—consistently with what has been said—lies out of our plan; whether a real history followed it, or the peoples in question never attained a political constitu-

tion.—It is a great discovery in history—as of a new world—which
has been made within rather more than the last twenty years,
respecting the Sanscrit and the connection of the European languages with it. In particular, the connection of the German and
Indian peoples has been demonstrated, with as much certainty
as such subjects allow of. Even at the present time we know of
peoples which scarcely form a society, much less a state, but that
have been long known as existing; while with regard to others,
which in their advanced condition excite our especial interest,
tradition reaches beyond the record of the founding of the state,
and they experienced many changes prior to that epoch. In the
connection just referred to, between the languages of nations so
widely separated, we have a result before us, which proves the
diffusion of those nations from Asia as a centre, and the so dis-
similar development of what had been originally related, as an
incontestable fact; not *as* an inference deduced by that favourite
method of combining, and reasoning from, circumstances grave
and trivial, which has already enriched and will continue to
enrich history with so many fictions given out as facts. But that
apparently so extensive range of events lies beyond the pale of
history; in fact preceded it.

In our language the term history[1] unites the objective with the
subjective side, and denotes quite as much the *historia rerum
gestarum*, as the *res gestae* themselves; on the other hand it comprehends not less what has *happened*, than the *narration* of what
has happened. This union of the two meanings we must regard as
of a higher order than mere outward accident; we must suppose
historical narrations to have appeared contemporaneously with
historical deeds and events. It is an internal vital principle common to both that produces them synchronously. Family memorials,
patriarchal traditions, have an interest confined to the family and
the clan. The uniform course of events which such a condition
implies, is no subject of serious remembrance; though distinct
transactions or turns of fortune, may rouse Mnemosyne to form
conceptions of them,—in the same way as love and the religious
emotions provoke imagination to give shape to a previously formless impulse. But it is the state which first presents subject-matter

[1] German, "Geschichte," from "geschehen," to happen.

that is not only *adapted* to the prose of history, but involves the production of such history in the very progress of its own being. Instead of merely subjective mandates on the part of government, —sufficing for the needs of the moment,—a community that is acquiring a stable existence, and exalting itself into a state, requires formal commands and laws—comprehensive and universally binding prescriptions; and thus produces a record as well as an interest concerned with intelligent, definite—and, in their results—lasting transactions and occurrences; on which Mnemosyne, for the behoof of the perennial object of the formation and constitution of the state, is impelled to confer perpetuity. Profound sentiments generally, such as that of love, as also religious intuition and its conceptions, are in themselves complete—constantly present and satisfying; but that outward existence of a political constitution which is enshrined in its rational laws and customs, is an *imperfect* present; and cannot be thoroughly understood without a knowledge of the past.

The periods—whether we suppose them to be centuries or millennia—that were passed by nations before history was written among them,—and which may have been filled with revolutions, nomadic wanderings, and the strangest mutations,—are on that very account destitute of *objective* history, because they present no *subjective* history, no annals. We need not suppose that the records of such periods have accidentally perished; rather, because they were not possible, do we find them wanting. Only in a state cognizant of laws, can distinct transactions take place, accompanied by such a clear consciousness of them as supplies the ability and suggests the necessity of an enduring record. It strikes every one, in beginning to form an acquaintance with the treasures of Indian literature, that a land so rich in intellectual products, and those of the profoundest order of thought, has no history; and in this respect contrasts most strongly with China—an empire possessing one so remarkable, one going back to the most ancient times. India has not only ancient books relating to religion, and splendid poetical productions, but also ancient codes; the existence of which latter kind of literature has been mentioned as a condition necessary to the origination of history—and yet history itself is not found. But in that country the impulse of organization, in beginning to develop social distinctions, was immediately petrified in the merely natural classification according to *castes;* so that although the laws concern themselves with civil rights, they make even these dependent on natural distinctions; and are especially occupied with determining the relations (wrongs rather than rights) of those classes towards each other, *i.e.*, the privileges of the higher over the lower. Consequently, the element of morality is banished from the pomp of Indian life and from its political institutions. Where that iron bondage of distinctions derived from nature prevails, the connection of society is nothing but wild arbitrariness,—transient activity,—or rather the play of violent emotion without any goal of advancement or development. Therefore no intelligent reminiscence, no object for Mnemosyne presents itself; and imagination—confused though profound—expatiates in a region, which, to be capable of history, must have had an aim within the domain of actuality, and, at the same time, of substantial freedom.

Since such are the conditions indispensable to a history, it has happened that the growth of families to clans, of clans to peoples, and their local diffusion consequent upon this numerical increase, —a series of facts which itself suggests so many instances of social complication, war, revolution, and ruin,—a process which is so rich in interest, and so comprehensive in extent,—has occurred without giving rise to history: moreover, that the extension and organic growth of the empire of articulate sounds has itself remained voiceless and dumb,—a stealthy, unnoticed advance. It is a fact revealed by philological monuments, that languages, during a rude condition of the nations that have spoken them, have been very highly developed; that the human understanding occupied this theoretical region with great ingenuity and completeness. For grammar, in its extended and consistent form, is the work of thought, which makes its categories distinctly visible therein. It is, moreover, a fact, that with advancing social and political civilization, this systematic completeness of intelligence suffers attrition, and language thereupon becomes poorer and ruder: a singular phenomenon—that the progress towards a more highly intellectual condition, while expanding and cultivating rationality, should disregard that intelligent amplitude and expressiveness—should find it an obstruction and contrive to do without it. Speech is the act of theoretic intelligence in a special sense; it is its *external* manifestation. Exercises of memory and imagination, without language, are direct, [non-speculative] manifestations. But this act of theoretic intelligence itself, as also its subsequent development, and the more concrete class of facts connected with it,—viz. the spreading of peoples over the earth, their separation from each other, their comminglings and wanderings—remain involved in the obscurity of a voiceless past. They are not acts of will becoming self-conscious—of freedom, mirroring itself in a phenomenal form, and creating for itself a proper actuality. Not partaking of this element of substantial, veritable existence, those nations—notwithstanding the development of language among them—never advanced to the possession of a *history*. The rapid growth of language, and the progress and dispersion of nations, assume importance and interest for concrete Reason, only when they have come in contact with states, or begin to form political constitutions themselves.

After these remarks, relating to the form of the *commencement* of the world's history, and to that ante-historical period which must be excluded from it, we have to state the direction of its course: though here only formally. The further definition of the subject in the concrete, comes under the head of arrangement.

Universal history—as already demonstrated—shews the development of the consciousness of freedom on the part of Spirit, and of the consequent realization of that freedom. This development implies a gradation—a series of increasingly adequate expressions or manifestations of freedom, which result from its Idea. The logical, and—as still more prominent—the *dialectical* nature of the Idea in general, viz. that it is self-determined—that it assumes successive forms which it successively transcends; and by this very process of transcending its earlier stages, gains an affirmative, and, in fact, a richer and more concrete shape;—this necessity of its nature, and the necessary series of pure abstract forms which the Idea successively assumes—is exhibited in the department of logic. Here we need adopt only one of its results, viz. that every step in the process, as differing from any other, has its determinate peculiar principle. In history this principle is idiosyncrasy of Spirit— peculiar national genius. It is within the limitations of this idiosyncrasy that the spirit of the nation, concretely manifested, expresses every aspect of its consciousness and will—the whole cycle

THE PHILOSOPHY OF HISTORY

of its realization. Its religion, its polity, its ethics, its legislation, and even its science, art, and mechanical skill, all bear its stamp. These special peculiarities find their key in that common peculiarity,—the particular principle that characterises a people; as, on the other hand, in the facts which history presents in detail, that common characteristic principle may be detected. That such or such a specific quality constitutes the peculiar genius of a people, is the element of our inquiry which must be derived from experience, and historically proved. To accomplish this, pre-supposes not only a disciplined faculty of abstraction, but an intimate acquaintance with the Idea. The investigator must be familiar *à priori* (if we like to call it so), with the whole circle of conceptions to which the principles in question belong—just as Keppler (to name the most illustrious example in this mode of philosophizing) must have been familiar *à priori* with ellipses, with cubes and squares, and with ideas of their relations, before he could discover, from the empirical data, those immortal "laws" of his, which are none other than forms of thought pertaining to those classes of conceptions. He who is unfamiliar with the science that embraces these abstract elementary conceptions, is as little capable —though he may have gazed on the firmament and the motions of the celestial bodies for a life-time—of *understanding* those laws, as of *discovering* them. From this want of acquaintance with the ideas that relate to the development of freedom, proceed a part of those objections which are brought against the philosophical consideration of a science usually regarded as one of mere experience; the so-called *à priori* method, and the attempt to insinuate ideas into the empirical data of history, being the chief points in the indictment. Where this deficiency exists, such conceptions appear alien—not lying within the object of investigation. To minds whose training has been narrow and merely subjective,— which have not an acquaintance and familiarity with ideas,—they are something strange—not embraced in the notion and conception of the subject which their limited intellect forms. Hence the statement that philosophy does not understand such sciences. It must, indeed, allow that it has not that kind of understanding which is the prevailing one in the domain of those sciences, that it does not proceed according to the categories of such understanding, but according to the categories of *Reason*—though at the same time recognising that Understanding, and its true value and position. It must be observed that in this very process of scientific *understanding,* it is of importance that the essential should be distinguished and brought into relief in contrast with the so-called non-essential. But in order to render this possible, we must know what *is essential;* and that is—in view of the history of the world in general—the consciousness of freedom, and the phases which this consciousness assumes in developing itself. The bearing of historical facts on this category, is their bearing on the truly essential. Of the difficulties stated, and the opposition exhibited to comprehensive conceptions in science, part must be referred to the inability to grasp and understand ideas. If in natural history some monstrous hybrid growth is alleged as an objection to the recognition of clear and indubitable classes or species, a sufficient reply is furnished by a sentiment often vaguely urged,—that "the exception confirms the rule;" *i.e.,* that is the part of a well-defined rule, to shew the conditions in which it applies, or the deficiency or hybridism of cases that are abnormal. Mere nature is too weak to keep its genera and species pure, when conflicting with alien elementary influences. If, *e.g.,* on considering the human organization in its concrete aspect, we assert that brain, heart, and so forth are essential to its organic life, some miserable abortion may be adduced, which has on the whole the human form, or parts of it,—which has been conceived in a human body and has breathed after birth therefrom,—in which nevertheless no brain and no heart is found. If such an instance is quoted against the general conception of a human being—the objector persisting in using the name, coupled with a superficial idea respecting it— it can be proved that a real, concrete human being, is a truly different object; that such a being must have a brain in its head, and a heart in its breast.

A similar process of reasoning is adopted, in reference to the correct assertion that genius, talent, moral virtues, and sentiments, and piety, may be found in every zone, under all political constitutions and conditions; in confirmation of which examples are forthcoming in abundance. If in this assertion, the accompanying distinctions are intended to be repudiated as unimportant or nonessential, reflection evidently limits itself to abstract categories; and ignores the particulars of the object in question, which certainly fall under no principle recognised by such categories. That intellectual position which adopts such merely .formal points of view, presents a vast field for ingenious questions, erudite views, and striking comparisons; for profound seeming reflections and declamations, which may be rendered so much the more brilliant in proportion as the subject they refer to is indefinite, and are susceptible of new and varied forms in inverse proportion to the importance of the results that can be gained from them, and the certainty and rationality of their issues. Under such an aspect the well known Indian epopees may be compared with the Homeric; perhaps—since it is the vastness of the imagination by which poetical genius proves itself—preferred to them; as, on account of the similarity of single strokes of imagination in the attributes of the divinities, it has been contended that Greek mythological forms may be recognised in those of India. Similarly the Chinese philosophy, as adopting the One [tōen] as its basis, has been alleged to be the same as at a later period appeared as Eleatic philosophy and as the Spinozistic system; while in virtue of its expressing itself also in abstract numbers and lines, Pythagorean and Christian principles have been supposed to be detected in it. Instances of bravery and indomitable courage,—traits of magnanimity, of self-denial, and self-sacrifice, which are found among the most savage and the most pusillanimous nations,—are regarded as sufficient to support the view that in these nations as much of social virtue and morality may be found as in the most civilized Christian states, or even more. And on this ground a doubt has been suggested whether in the progress of history and of general culture mankind have become better; whether their morality has been increased,—morality being regarded in a subjective aspect and view, as founded on what the agent holds to be right and wrong, good and evil; not on a principle which is considered to be in and for itself right and good, or a crime and evil, or on a particular religion believed to be the true one.

We may fairly decline on this occasion the task of tracing the formalism and error of such a view, and establishing the true principles of morality, or rather of social virtue in opposition to false morality. For the history of the world occupies a higher ground than that on which morality has properly its position, which is personal character,—the conscience of individuals,—their particular will and mode of action; *these* have a value, imputation, reward or punishment proper to themselves. What the absolute aim of Spirit requires and accomplishes,—what providence does,— transcends the obligations, and the liability to imputation and the ascription of good or bad motives, which attach to individuality in virtue of its social relations. They who on moral grounds, and consequently with noble intention, have resisted that which the advance of the spiritual Idea makes necessary, stand higher in moral worth than those whose crimes have been turned into the means—under the direction of a superior principle—of realising the purposes of that principle. But in such revolutions both parties generally stand within the limits of the same circle of transient and corruptible existence. Consequently it is only a formal rectitude—deserted by the living Spirit and by God—which those who stand upon ancient right and order maintain. The deeds of great men, who are the Individuals of the world's history, thus appear not only justified in view of that intrinsic result of which they were not conscious, but also from the point of view occupied by the secular moralist. But looked at from this point, moral claims that are irrelevant, must not be brought into collision with world-historical deeds and their accomplishment. The litany of private virtues—modesty, humility, philanthropy and forbearance—must not be raised against them. The history of the world might, on principle, entirely ignore the circle within which morality and the so much talked of distinction between the moral and the politic lies—not only in abstaining from judgments, for the principles involved, and the necessary reference of the deeds in question to those principles, are a sufficient judgment of them—but in leaving individuals quite out of view and unmentioned. What it has to record is the activity of the spirit of peoples, so that the individual forms which that spirit has assumed in the sphere of outward actuality, might be left to the delineation of special histories.

The same kind of formalism avails itself in its peculiar manner of the indefiniteness attaching to genius, poetry, and even philosophy; thinks equally that it finds these everywhere. We have here products of reflective thought; and it is familiarity with those general conceptions which single out and name real distinctions without fathoming the true depth of the matter,—that we call culture. It is something merely formal, inasmuch as it aims at nothing more than the analysis of the subject, whatever it be, into its constituent parts, and the comprehension of these in their logical definitions and forms. It is not the free universality of conception necessary for making an abstract principle the object of consciousness. Such a consciousness of thought itself, and of its forms isolated from a particular object, is philosophy. This has, indeed, the condition of its existence in culture; that condition being the taking up of the object of thought, and at the same time clothing it with the form of universality, in such a way that the material content and the form given by the intellect are held in an inseparable state;—inseparable to such a degree that the object in question—which, by the analysis of one conception into a multitude of conceptions, is enlarged to an incalculable treasure of thought—is regarded as a merely empirical datum in whose formation thought has had no share.

But it is quite as much an act of thought—of the understanding in particular—to embrace in one simple conception an object which of itself comprehends a concrete and large significance (as earth, man,—Alexander or Caesar) and to designate it by one word,—as to *resolve* such a conception—duly to isolate in idea the conceptions which it contains, and to give them particular names. And in reference to the view which gave occasion to what has just been said, thus much will be clear,—that as reflection produces what we include under the general terms genius, talent, art, science,— formal culture on every grade of intellectual development, not only can, but must grow, and attain a mature bloom, while the grade in question is developing itself to a state, and on this basis of civilization is advancing to intelligent reflection and to general forms of thought,—as in laws, so in regard to all else. In the very association of men in a state, lies the necessity of formal culture— consequently of the rise of the sciences and of a cultivated poetry and art generally. The arts designated "plastic," require besides, even in their technical aspects, the civilized association of men. The poetic art—which has less need of external requirements and means, and which has the element of immediate existence, the voice, as its material—steps forth with great boldness and with matured expression, even under the conditions presented by a people not yet united in a political combination; since, as re- marked above, language attains on its own particular ground a high intellectual development, prior to the commencement of civilization.

Philosophy also must make its appearance where political life exists; since that in virtue of which any series of phenomena is reduced within the spheres of culture, as above stated, is the form strictly proper to thought; and thus for philosophy, which is nothing other than the consciousness of this form itself—the thinking of thinking,—the material of which its edifice is to be constructed, is already prepared by *general* culture. If in the development of the state itself, periods are necessitated which impel the soul of nobler natures to seek refuge from the present in ideal regions,—in order to find in them that harmony with itself which it can no longer enjoy in the discordant real world, where the reflective intelligence attacks all that is holy and deep, which had been spontaneously inwrought into the religion, laws and manners of nations, and brings them down and attenuates them to abstract godless generalities,—thought will be compelled to become thinking Reason, with the view of effecting in its own element, the restoration of its principles from the ruin to which they had been brought.

We find then, it is true, among all world-historical peoples, poetry, plastic art, science, even philosophy; but not only is there a diversity in style and bearing generally, but still more remarkably in subject-matter; and this is a diversity of the most important kind, affecting the rationality of that subject-matter. It is useless for a pretentious aesthetic criticism to demand that our good pleasure should not be made to rule for the matter—the substantial part of their contents—and to maintain that it is the beautiful form as such, the grandeur of the fancy, and so forth, which fine art aims at, and which must be considered and enjoyed by a liberal taste and cultivated mind. A healthy intellect does not tolerate such abstractions, and cannot assimilate productions of the kind above referred to. Granted that the Indian epopees might be placed on a level with the Homeric, on account of a number of those qualities of form—grandeur of invention and imaginative power, liveliness of images and emotions, and beauty of diction; yet the infinite difference of matter remains; consequently one of substantial importance and involving the interest of Reason, which is immediately concerned with the consciousness of the idea of freedom, and its expression in individuals. There is not only a classical *form*, but a classical order of *subject-matter;* and in a work of art form and subject-matter are so closely united that the former can only be classical to the extent to which the latter is so. With a fantastical, indeterminate material—the *rule* is the essence of *Reason*—the form becomes measureless and formless, or mean and contracted. In the same way, in that comparison of the various systems of philosophy of which we have already spoken, the only point of importance is overlooked, namely, the character of that unity which is found alike in the Chinese, the Eleatic, and the Spinozistic philosophy—the distinction between the recognition of that unity as abstract and as concrete—concrete to the extent of being a unity in and by itself—a unity synonymous with Spirit. But that co-ordination proves that it recognises only such an abstract unity; so that while it gives judgment respecting philosophy, it is ignorant of that very point which constitutes the interest of philosophy.

But there are also spheres which, amid all the variety that is presented in the substantial content of a particular form of culture, remain the same. The difference above mentioned in art, science, philosophy, concerns the thinking Reason and freedom, which is the self-consciousness of the former, and which has the same one root with thought. As it is not the brute, but only the man that thinks, he only—and only because he is a thinking being—has freedom. *His* consciousness imports this, that the individual comprehends itself as a *person*, that is, recognises itself in its single existence as possessing universality,—as capable of abstraction from, and of surrendering all speciality; and, therefore, as inherently infinite. Consequently those spheres of intelligence which lie beyond the limits of this consciousness are a common ground among those substantial distinctions. Even morality, which is so intimately connected with the consciousness of freedom, can be very pure while that consciousness is still wanting; as far, that is to say, as it expresses duties and rights only as *objective* commands; or even as far as it remains satisfied with the merely formal elevation of the soul—the surrender of the sensual, and of all sensual motives—in a purely negative, self-denying fashion. The *Chinese* morality—since Europeans have become acquainted with it and with the writings of Confucius—has obtained the greatest praise and proportionate attention from those who are familiar with the Christian morality. There is a similar acknowledgement of the sublimity with which the *Indian* religion and poetry, (a statement that must, however, be limited to the higher kind), but especially the Indian philosophy, expatiate upon and demand the removal and sacrifice of sensuality. Yet both these nations are, it must be confessed, *entirely* wanting in the essential consciousness of the idea of freedom. To the Chinese their moral laws are just like natural laws,—external, positive commands,—claims established by force,—compulsory duties or rules of courtesy towards each other. Freedom, through which alone the essential determinations of Reason become moral sentiments, is wanting. Morality is a political affair, and its laws are administered by officers of government and legal tribunals. Their treatises upon it (which are not law books, but are certainly addressed to the subjective will and individual disposition) read,—as do the moral writings of the Stoics,—like a string of commands stated as necessary for realising the goal of happiness; so that it seems to be left free to men, on their part, to adopt such commands,—to observe them or not; while the conception of an abstract subject, "a wise man" [sapiens] forms the culminating point among the Chinese, as also among the Stoic moralists. Also in the Indian doctrine of the renunciation of the sensuality of desires and earthly interests, positive moral freedom is not the object and end, but the annihilation of consciousness—spiritual and even physical privation of life.

It is the concrete spirit of a people which we have distinctly to recognise, and since it is Spirit it can only be comprehended spiritually, that is, by thought. It is this alone which takes the lead in all the deeds and tendencies of that people, and which is occupied in realising itself,—in satisfying its ideal and becoming self-conscious,—for its great business is self-production. But for spirit, the highest attainment is self-knowledge; an advance not only to the *intuition*, but to the *thought*—the clear conception of itself. This it must and is also destined to accomplish; but the accomplishment is at the same time its dissolution, and the rise of another spirit, another world-historical people, another epoch of universal history. This transition and connection leads us to the connection of the whole—the idea of the world's history as such—which we have now to consider more closely, and of which we have to give a representation.

History in general is therefore the development of Spirit in *time,* as nature is the development of the Idea in *space.*

If then we cast a glance over the world's history generally, we see a vast picture of changes and transactions; of infinitely manifold forms of peoples, states, individuals, in unresting succession. Everything that can enter into and interest the soul of man—all our sensibility to *goodness, beauty, and greatness*—is called into play. On every hand aims are adopted and pursued, which we recognise, whose accomplishment we desire—we hope and fear for them. In all these occurrences and changes we behold human action and suffering predominant; everywhere something akin to ourselves, and therefore everywhere something that excites our interest for or against. Sometimes it attracts us by beauty, freedom, and rich variety, sometimes by energy such as enables even vice to make itself interesting. Sometimes we see the more comprehensive mass of some general interest advancing with comparative slowness, and subsequently sacrificed to an infinite complication of trifling circumstances, and so dissipated into atoms. Then, again, with a vast expenditure of power a trivial result is produced; while from what appears unimportant a tremendous issue proceeds. On every hand there is the motliest throng of events drawing us within the circle of its interest, and when one combination vanishes another immediately appears in its place.

The general thought—the category which first presents itself in this restless mutation of individuals and peoples, existing for a time and then vanishing—is that of *change* at large. The sight of the ruins of some ancient sovereignty directly leads us to contemplate this thought of change in its negative aspect. What traveller among the ruins of Carthage, of Palmyra, Persepolis, or Rome, has not been stimulated by reflections on the transiency of kingdoms and men, and to sadness at the thought of a vigorous and rich life now departed—a sadness which does not expend itself on personal losses and the uncertainty of one's own undertakings, but is a disinterested sorrow at the decay of a splendid and highly cultured national life! But the next consideration which allics itself with that of change, is, that change while it imports dissolution, involves at the same time the rise of a *new life*—that while death is the issue of life, life is also the issue of death. This is a grand conception; one which the Oriental thinkers attained, and which is perhaps the highest in their metaphysics. In the idea of *metempsychosis* we find it evolved in its relation to individual existence; but a myth more generally known, is that of the *Phoenix* as a type of the life of *nature;* eternally preparing for itself its funeral pile, and consuming itself upon it; but so that from its ashes is produced the new, renovated, fresh life. But this image is only Asiatic; oriental not occidental. Spirit—consuming the envelope of its existence—does not merely pass into another envelope, nor rise rejuvenescent from the ashes of its previous form; it comes forth exalted, glorified, a purer spirit. It certainly makes war upon itself—consumes its own existence; but in this very destruction it works up that existence into a new form, and each successive phase becomes in its turn a material, working on which it exalts itself to a new grade.

If we consider Spirit in this aspect—regarding its changes not merely as rejuvenescent transitions, *i.e.,* returns to the same form, but rather as manipulations of itself, by which it multiplies the material for future endeavours—we see it exerting itself in a variety of modes and directions; developing its powers and grati-fying its desires in a variety which is inexhaustible; because every one of its creations, in which it has already found gratification, meets it anew as material, and is a new stimulus to plastic activity. The abstract conception of mere change gives place to the thought of Spirit manifesting, developing, and perfecting its powers in every direction which its manifold nature can follow. What powers it inherently possesses we learn from the variety of products and formations which it originates. In this pleasurable activity, it has to do only with itself. As involved with the conditions of mere nature—internal and external—it will indeed meet in these not only opposition and hindrance, but will often see its endeavours thereby fail; often sink under the complications in which it is entangled either by nature or by itself. But in such case it perishes in fulfilling its own destiny and proper function, and even thus exhibits the spectacle of self-demonstration as spiritual activity.

The very essence of Spirit is activity; it actualizes its potentiality —makes itself its own deed, its own work—and thus becomes an object to itself; contemplates itself as an objective existence. Thus is it with the Spirit of a people: it is a Spirit having strictly defined characteristics, which erects itself into an objective world, that exists and persists in a particular religious form of worship, customs, constitution and political laws,—in the whole complex of its institutions,—in the events and transactions that make up its history. That is its work—that is what this particular nation *is*. Nations are what their deeds are. Every Englishman will say: We are the men who navigate the ocean, and have the commerce of the world; to whom the East Indies belong and their riches; who have a parliament, juries, &c.—The relation of the individual to that Spirit is that he appropriates to himself this substantial existence; that it becomes his character and capability, enabling him to have a definite place in the world—to be *something*. For he finds the being of the people to which he belongs an already established, firm world—objectively present to him—with which he has to incorporate himself. In this its work, therefore—its world—the spirit of the people enjoys its existence and finds its satisfaction.—A nation is moral—virtuous—vigorous—while it is engaged in realising its grand objects, and defends its work against external violence during the process of giving to its purposes an objective existence. The contradiction between its potential, subjective being—its inner aim and life—and its *actual* being is removed; it has attained full actuality, has itself objectively present to it. But this having been attained, the activity displayed by the Spirit of the people in question is no longer needed; it has its desire. The nation can still accomplish much in war and peace at home and abroad; but the living substantial soul itself may be said to have ceased its activity. The essential, supreme interest has consequently vanished from its life, for interest is present only where there is opposition. The nation lives the same kind of life as the individual when passing from maturity to old age,—in the enjoyment of itself,—in the satisfaction of being exactly what it desired and was able to attain. Although its imagination might have transcended that limit, it nevertheless abandoned any such aspirations as objects of *actual endeavour*, if the real world was less than favourable to their attainment—and restricted its aim by the conditions thus imposed. This mere *customary life* (the watch wound up and going on of itself) is that which brings on natural death. Custom is activity without opposition, for which there remains only a formal duration; in which the fulness and zest that originally characterised the aim of life is out of the question,—a merely external sensuous existence which has ceased to throw itself enthusiastically into its object. Thus perish individuals, thus perish peoples by a natural death; and though the latter may continue in being, it is an existence without intellect or vitality; having no need of its institutions, because the need for them is satisfied,—a political nullity and tedium. In order that a truly universal interest may arise, the spirit of a people must advance to the adoption of some new purpose: but whence can this new purpose originate? It would be a higher, more comprehensive conception of itself—a transcending of its principle—but this very act would involve a principle of a new order, a new national spirit.

Such a new principle does in fact enter into the spirit of a people that has arrived at full development and self-realization; it dies not a simply natural death,—for it is not a mere single individual, but a spiritual, generic life; in its case natural death appears to imply destruction through its own agency. The reason of this difference from the single natural individual, is that the spirit of a people exists as a *genus,* and consequently carries within it its own negation, in the very generality which characterises it. A people can only die a violent death when it has become naturally dead in itself, as *e.g.,* the German imperial cities, the German imperial constitution.

It is not of the nature of the all-pervading Spirit to die this merely natural death; it does not simply sink into the senile life of mere custom, but—as being a national spirit belonging to universal history—attains to the consciousness of what its work is; it attains to a conception of itself. In fact, it is world-historical only in so far as a *universal principle* has lain in its fundamental element,—in its grand aim: only so far is the work which such a spirit produces, a moral, political organization. If it be mere desires that impel nations to activity, such deeds pass over without leaving a trace; or their traces are only ruin and destruction. Thus, it was first Chronos—Time—that ruled; the Golden Age, without moral products; and what was produced—the offspring of that Chronos—was devoured by it. It was Jupiter—from whose head Minerva sprang, and to whose circle of divinities belong Apollo and the Muses—that first put a constraint upon time, and set a bound to its principle of decadence. He is the political god, who produced a moral work—the state.

In the very element of an achievement the quality of generality, of thought, is contained; without thought it has no objectivity; that is its basis. The highest point in the development of a people is this,—to have gained a conception of its life and condition,—to have reduced its laws, its idea of justice and morality to a science; for in this unity [of the objective and subjective] lies the most intimate unity that Spirit can attain to in and with itself. In its work it is employed in rendering itself an object of its own contemplation; but it cannot develop itself objectively in its essential nature, except in *thinking* itself.

At this point, then, Spirit is acquainted with its principles—the general character of its acts. But at the same time, in virtue of its very generality, this work of thought is different in point of form from the actual achievements of the national genius, and from the vital agency by which those achievements have been performed. We have then before us a *real* and an *ideal* existence of the spirit of the nation. If we wish to gain the general idea and conception of what the Greeks were, we find it in Sophocles and Aristophanes, in Thucydides and Plato. In these individuals the Greek spirit conceived and thought itself. This is the profounder kind of satisfaction which the spirit of a people attains; but it is "ideal," and distinct from its "real" activity.

At such a time, therefore, we are sure to see a people finding satisfaction in the *idea* of virtue; putting *talk* about virtue partly side by side with actual virtue, but partly in the place of it. On the other hand pure, universal thought, since its nature is universality, is apt to bring the special and spontaneous—belief, trust, customary morality—to reflect upon itself, and its primitive simplicity; to shew up the limitation with which it is fettered,—partly suggesting reasons for renouncing duties, partly itself *demanding reasons*, and the connection of such requirements with universal thought; and not finding that connection, seeking to impeach the authority of duty generally, as destitute of a sound foundation.

At the same time the isolation of individuals from each other and from the whole makes its appearance; their aggressive selfishness and vanity; their seeking personal advantage and consulting this at the expense of the state at large. That inward principle in transcending its outward manifestations is subjective also in *form* —viz., selfishness and corruption in the unbound passions and egotistic interests of men.

Zeus, therefore, who is represented as having put a limit to the devouring agency of time, and staid this transiency by having established something inherently and independently durable— Zeus and his race are themselves swallowed up, and that by the very power that produced them—the principle of thought, perception, reasoning, insight derived from rational grounds, and the requirement of such grounds.

Time is the negative element in the sensuous world. Thought is the same negativity, but it is the deepest, the infinite form of it, in which therefore all existence generally is dissolved; first *finite* existence,—*determinate*, limited form: but existence *generally*, in its objective character, is limited; it appears therefore as a mere datum—something immediate—authority:—and is either intrinsically finite and limited, or presents itself as a limit for the thinking subject, and its infinite reflection on itself [unlimited abstraction].

But first we must observe how the life which proceeds from death, is itself, on the other hand, only individual life; so that, regarding the species as the real and substantial in this vicissitude, the perishing of the individual is a regress of the species into individuality. The perpetuation of the race is, therefore, none other than the monotonous repetition of the same kind of existence. Further, we must remark how perception,—the comprehension of being by thought,—is the source and birthplace of a new, and in fact higher form, in a principle which while it preserves, dignifies its material. For thought is that *universal*—that *species* which is immortal, which preserves identity with itself. The particular form of Spirit not merely passes away in the world by natural causes in time, but is annulled in the automatic self-mirroring activity of consciousness. Because this annulling is an activity of thought, it is at the same time conservative and elevating in its operation. While then, on the one side, Spirit annuls the reality, the permanence of that which it *is*, it gains on the other side, the essence, the thought, the universal element of that which *it only was* [its transient conditions]. Its principle is no longer that immediate import and aim which it was previously, but the *essence* of that import and aim.

The result of this process is then that Spirit, in rendering itself objective and making this its being an object of thought, on the one hand destroys the determinate form of its being, on the other hand gains a comprehension of the universal element which it involves, and thereby gives a new form to its inherent principle. In virtue of this, the substantial character of the national spirit has been altered,—that is, its principle has risen into another, and in fact a higher principle.

It is of the highest importance in apprehending and comprehending history to have and to understand the thought involved in this transition. The individual traverses as a unity various grades of development, and remains the same individual; in like manner also does a people, till the Spirit which it embodies reaches the grade of universality. In this point lies the fundamental, the ideal necessity of transition. This is the soul—the essential consideration—of the philosophical comprehension of history.

Spirit is essentially the result of its own activity; its activity is the transcending of immediate, simple, unreflected existence,—the negation of that existence, and the returning into itself. We may compare it with the seed; for with this the plant begins, yet it is also the result of the plant's entire life. But the weak side of life is exhibited in the fact that the commencement and the result are disjoined from each other. Thus also is it in the life of individuals and peoples. The life of a people ripens a certain fruit; its activity aims at the complete manifestation of the principle which it embodies. But this fruit does not fall back into the bosom of the people that produced and matured it; on the contrary, it becomes a poison-draught to it. That poison-draught it cannot let alone, for it has an insatiable thirst for it: the taste of the draught is its annihilation, though at the same time the rise of a new principle.

We have already discussed the final aim of progression. The principles of the successive phases of Spirit that animate the nations in a necessitated gradation, are themselves only steps in the development of the one universal Spirit, which through them elevates and completes itself to a self-comprehending *totality*.

While we are thus concerned exclusively with the idea of Spirit, and in the history of the world regard everything as only its manifestation, we have, in traversing the past,—however extensive its periods,—only to do with what is *present;* for philosophy, as occupying itself with the true, has to do with the *eternally present.* Nothing in the past is lost for it, for the Idea is ever present; Spirit is immortal; with it there is no past, no future, but an essential *now.* This necessarily implies that the present form of Spirit comprehends within it all earlier steps. These have indeed unfolded themselves in succession independently; but what Spirit is it has always been essentially; distinctions are only the development of this essential nature. The life of the ever present Spirit is a circle of progressive embodiments, which looked at in one respect still exist beside each other, and only as looked at from another point of view appear as past. The grades which Spirit seems to have left behind it, it still possesses in the depths of its present.